ARE WE REALLY
FRIENDS?

ARE WE REALLY
FRIENDS?
The Road to Godly Friendship!

Dr. Patricia McLeod

XULON PRESS

Xulon Press
2301 Lucien Way #415
Maitland, FL 32751
407.339.4217
www.xulonpress.com

Unless otherwise indicated, Scripture quotations taken from the King James Version (KJV)–*public domain*.

Scripture quotations taken from the Holy Bible, New Living Translation (NLT). Copyright ©1996, 2004, 2007 by Tyndale House Foundation. Used by permission of Tyndale House Publishers, Inc.

Scripture quotations taken from the Holy Bible, New International Version (NIV). Copyright © 1973, 1978, 1984, 2011 by Biblica, Inc.™. Used by permission. All rights reserved.

Printed in the United States of America.

ISBN-13: 978-1-6312-9796-0
Ebook: ISBN-13: 978-1-6312-9797-7

Acknowledgments

I'd like to thank my beloved Bishop Jacqueline E. McCullough for goading me into this study. It is because of her keen sensitivity and discernment that she challenged me to this work. She encouraged me to filter my thoughts about friendship through the Scriptures, so I could be healed. Thank you for your faithful commitment as my Shepherd.

I'd like to thank my friend and confidant, Overseer Robyn Edwards for walking me through the many layers of issues that unfold when examining friendships. It was in these in-depth discussions that we both acknowledged God was calling this work to be a book. It is our prayer that many will be healed as a result. Thanks for being the consummate counselor and friend that you are.

I'd like to thank my twin Bishop Julia McMillan, and dear friend, Pastor Kanyere Eaton for encouraging me to stay the course! Every time I felt like quitting, they seemed to always be there with a Word from the Lord that kept me focused and relenting in the work. I thank God He has given you both to me as sisters, friends and confidants for life!

I'd like to thank my husband, General, for his patience and support throughout this process. What a kind and generous person you are. I appreciate your consistency and endurance, love, and reassurance. I am forever grateful for your lifelong commitment, and I am so proud to call you my husband.

Finally, I'd like to thank my Lord and Savior Jesus Christ for His direction and faithfulness. He truly inspired every word, every Scripture, every story, and every testimony recorded in these pages. This project simply would not have happened without His clear instructions and divine influence throughout the process. I am eternally grateful and humbled to have been chosen to record this work in honor of His name.

Table of Contents

Foreword

Friendship covers every area of our lives. Friends from the past, friends in the present, and friends in the future will influence and shape our lives forever. The subject of friendship has been pressed on Rev. Patricia McLeod's heart as she journeyed through Scripture and analyzed her own life using biblical text. The outcome of that Spirit-led walk birthed this book of enlightenment and guidance.

As you read, the light of God's Word, the healing of His presence, and the bonding of true friendship will become a reality in your life. This topic may have been thought about and many may have written about it. But this book, by God's design, will dig deep into the soul to expose buried pain and disappointment, misunderstanding, and variance. In turn, it will allow you to think harder, live more free, and embrace friendship. Read, grow, and enjoy!

Bishop Jacqueline E. McCullough

Introduction

This book may radically change the way you presently interact in friendships. It is designed to expose the demonic influence Satan has imposed on our friendships and offer our heavenly Father's blueprint to healthier relationships.

Severe outcomes are the result of unhealthy friendships. Competition, envy, suspicion, blame, and covetousness are a few examples. We have normalized these in our friendships because they are so common. Their presence in our relationships, however, was not intended by God. They are of Satan. Most of us follow Satan's demonic prescription for friendships because we are oblivious to his subtle influence. We assume we have a normal friendship but without the Lord at the center, healthy friendships are not possible. Who consults the Bible when they enter a friendship? Who prays to God to reveal His purpose for a particular friend? The answer is: Few of us do this. That is why this book is necessary. We will learn that friendships are either structured according to God's plan or destructive according to Satan's influence. There is no in between.

Before we proceed I'd like to invite any of you who are not saved or may have disconnected from the Lord, to commit your lives to Jesus Christ. This commitment not only assures you of eternal life with Him but will equip you with the Holy Spirit who gives us wisdom and guidance in all affairs of this life. If you confess your sins and truly believe in your heart that Jesus came to earth, suffered and died so you and I could live, and that God raised Jesus from the dead, then you shall be saved. Once you surrender your life to the Lord, the Holy Spirit will enter your heart and forever be with you on your road to righteousness and truth (Rom. 10:9–10, 1 John 1:9).

That doesn't mean you will be perfect, but, it does mean you will be in right standing with God and no longer live under the dominion and control of sin (Rom. 6:14). It means you will be empowered to hear the voice of God, receive His Word, and obey His instructions (John 10:27–28). This is the only way you and I will ever experience the joy of *true* friendships and relationships. It is impossible to embrace these sacred institutions without His Holy Spirit equipping us to live them out. Far too many of us have entered friendships and marriages that we confess in the presence of God, and then use the world's plan to try to make them work. Unfortunately, this is the reason so many of them fail. We're using the wrong manual!

This book is meant to liberate people from the bondage of erroneous beliefs about friendships. It is designed to exploit the false expectations we so readily impose on our friends so that we will refrain from unrealistic presuppositions. This work will also provide the biblical apologetic for God's design for friendships. Only then will we more easily recognize that any friendship not framed by God's design and purpose is dangerous and toxic. Lastly, this book will help you examine godly friendships with the hope of concluding that one of the greatest sources of spiritual strength is found in wholesome, Christian friendships.

For your further edification, I have included discussion questions at the end of each chapter. I encourage you to answer them privately and in group study. Be assured, greater enlightenment and healthier friendships will be your reward.

Rev. Dr. Patricia M. McLeod

Chapter One

True Friendships are a Gift from God

"Every good gift and every perfect gift is from above, and cometh down from the Father of lights, with whom is no variableness, neither shadow of turning" (James 1:17).

Have you ever felt like someone in your life was a gift from God? Do they contribute to the quality of your life in such a special way that they just *had* to come from God? We often describe these people as a "Godsend." We feel this way because it's true. Those people really are sent from God for His divine purposes. We are so blown away when this happens because, when those people come, it's always at the perfect time and they are able to provide exactly what we need. God, who knows our beginning from our end and knows every need in our lives, sent us exactly who we need in life. They are part of His divine plan to guide us in the direction we need to go. These people, who often become our most treasured friends, are really a gift from our loving Father.

Gifts are defined as "a thing given willingly without expectation of payment." The Cambridge Dictionary

1

reiterates this definition in this way: "something that is given without expectation of anything in return. Gifts are given to show affection. They can be given in the form of donations, contributions, or handouts, and are designed to bring joy."[1] A general consensus is that we give people gifts to show them we are grateful for them and value their role in our lives. With this general agreement, we begin to see that gifts send a message from the giver. The really exciting part about being a recipient of a gift is that the giver is usually not expecting any reciprocal treatment. The giver provides a gift out of perceived need, desire, or simply the kindness of their hearts. Most often, the giver has an appreciation and perhaps even a love for the recipient.

I want you to begin thinking about the last gift you received. Who gave it to you? Was it given out of pure intentions or did it come with strings attached? If there are strings attached, you have a problem. The giver's heart is not under the influence of God if they expect something in return. Even if the gift giver is a Christian, an ulterior motive is a sign that he or she may be influenced by Satan.

I chose James 1:17 as the verse for this chapter because James said that good and perfect gifts come from God. As we look at friends as gifts, they should be regarded as treasures from God. We can all agree that real friends have a true value in our lives. In my research on the value of friendship, I stumbled upon a very insightful article published in *Prague Leader's Magazine,* May 2009. Robert Stevenson wrote, "Friendship is indeed a gift, and a priceless one at that. And I would only be reiterating what many great minds have already said were I to try to describe the vitally important

---

[1] www.dictionary.cambridge.org.v "Gifts." The Cambridge English Dictionary.

role that friendship plays in our lives. To paraphrase Cicero, the importance of friendship is the only thing in the world about which all of mankind agree." [2] That said, let's examine the concept of friends as a gift.

The first use of the word "gift" in the Scripture from James 1:17, is translated from the Greek word *dosis* and denotes the act of giving. The word "good" which is used to describe the gift, means benevolent, profitable, and beneficial. It further signifies doing good to the benefit of others and implies friend or lover of good men. [3] When combined with the biblical definition of gift, we can interpret the verse to properly mean every beneficial, useful, upright and honorable act of giving comes from God!

The next use of the word "gift" in James 1:17 slightly differs from *dosis*. This instance is translated from the Greek word *dorema*, which means a gift, bounty, or benefaction. This means the recipient of the gift is automatically placed in the position to receive a perfect bounty or benefit; making the recipient a beneficiary. Many times, beneficiaries are blindsided by gifts they did not expect and they stand to benefit from something they did not do. The beneficiary is always placed in the position to live a more prosperous and stable life as a result of the gift.

I pray you will begin to scrutinize the benefits your friends bring to your life by asking if your life is more prosperous as a result of the relationship. My word of caution, however, is that "prosperous," in this context, does not examine the person based on the monetary gains they have

---

[2] *Coaching 4 Success; The Value of Friendship*; By Robert Lewis Stevenson. Prague Leader's Magazine; May 2009.

[3] The Key Word Greek / Hebrew Study Bible. "Good." Lexical Aids to the New Testament, Greek 18. James 1:17. AMG Publishers 1991.

provided in your life. Here, prosperous means enjoying vigorous and healthy growth.

The questions to ask yourself are:

1. Have you grown in your knowledge and understanding of God as a result of your friendships?

2. Do your friends edify you in the things of God?

If you answer "yes" to both those questions, then your friends are prospering your life. If you answered "no" to either of the questions above, then it's safe to conclude that friendship is not a gift from God. They're someone you've decided should be your friend. The Lord knows we have all been guilty of that. Too often when we meet people we are quick to determine they are someone that is meant for our lives. We get excited and develop high expectations for the relationship, often before we know anything about the person at all. I recall my teenage years when I would see a boy I thought I liked. My criteria was so superficial. It was always based upon how he looked, whether he was athletic or not, if he did well in school, and whether I thought he had some type of successful future. My attraction had nothing to do with whether the guy knew Jesus, whether he was morally astute, or whether he had knowledge of his purpose in the Lord.

We regularly determine if people should be our friends based upon visible commonalities, similar desires, and shared interests. If the connections are established based upon these superficial premises, they do not meet the criteria to be a gift from God. In my life, some of people were sent straight from Satan. He disguised them as people I could benefit, learn, and grow from. How could they not be? They looked how I wanted them to look. They had careers I approved of and aspirations that matched mine. I thought we would all rise to the top together! At the end of the day, those friends were people I forced to fit my worldly mold. When they inadequately met my needs, I felt angry and resentful toward them. I accused them of not being my true friends.

Those friendships leave us with tremendous disappointment, as well as feelings of rejection and mistrust. That is ultimately what Satan wants from these connections. He is so glad when we choose the wrong people to be friends with. They know nothing about how to support and encourage us in the things of God and they are far removed from our God-given purpose for living. There is no benefit to be gained from any friend who is not sent from God. The relationship is doomed from the start because ungodly friendships have no basis of what true friendship is and are not influenced by the Holy Spirit. Without the Bible and the Holy Spirit's influence in our friendships, we essentially have nothing; and that's what too many of us are settling for.

We are also guilty of settling for this emptiness in some marriages, regardless of whether two individuals are Christian or not. Too many people determine others to be their "soulmate" by using the same superficial, worldly premises we just discussed. I think it's very interesting that many Christians, who should know what the Bible says about marriage, purpose, etc., follow the same criteria as the world. Unfortunately, too often they enter into unholy alliances out of a determination to be satisfied according to their own standards; only to wake up in a destructive, ungodly, unhealthy relationship.

We must all learn to accept the truth found in Proverbs 19:21, which states, "Many are the plans in a person's heart, but it is the LORD'S purpose that prevails." If we learn to live governed by God's Word instead of our emotions and shallow opinions, then all the pain, disappointment, and anguish can be avoided. The distinction of God as "Lord" in the verse above, references God as *Jehovah*. *Jehovah* means God is a covenant keeping God who has a special commitment to care for His people. God sends the gift of friends and spouses because He knows who we need, when we need them, how long we need them, and why we need them. Life can become a nightmare if we decide to be God over our lives because we lack His wisdom, foresight, omniscience, and love.

God's gifts are good and perfect because they come from His unique love for us, which is a necessary component of true friendships. It is necessary because it loves beyond feelings and emotions and despite circumstances. God's love is based on purpose and comes solely from Him. Only the believer can experience the ability to love like this. 1 John 4:7 states, "Beloved, let us love one another, because love comes from God. Everyone who loves has been born of God, and knows God." The ability to love another person like God loves us is what makes friendships endure the test of time. His love equips relationships to stand under pressure and to endure the swift and often painful transitions of life. It is the glue that binds people's hearts together with chords that cannot be broken. It is the love that yields forgiveness, extends grace and mercy to the unlovable, and brings joy and hope to the downtrodden. Without God's love, known in the Greek language as *agape*, there can be no sustenance in friendships.

The exploitation of friendships and relationships began when Adam and Eve gave in to Satan's temptation. He exploited God's original intent for healthy relationships by releasing the spirits of blame, disharmony, competition, and greed. This all started when Adam and Eve ate of the fruit. Their harmonious relationship with God, and each other, was derailed. As a result, we are all born with an Adamic nature, which is a sin nature we inherited from Adam (1 Cor. 15:45). Subsequently, sinful acts have influenced our friendships and marriages causing us to often forfeit God's intention for lasting harmony and unity. When Adam and Eve lived under God's influence and in a right relationship with Him, competition, envy, blame, disrespect, hatred, and coveting didn't exist. After Adam and Eve's fall, an entirely different paradigm formed. Jealousy, resentment, discord, abuse, deception, and personal disregard began. These characteristics, all too common in many relationships, are unhealthy, ungodly, and contrary to God's precious gifts. His gifts are to be cherished not abused. They are to be harmonious and not filled with discord. Godly relationships are where persons are to be respected, not abused or disregarded. God's gifts are designed to mirror attributes that reflect the greatest gift ever given to mankind in friendship—Jesus Christ.

One of my most favorite times of the year is Christmas because we celebrate the birth of Jesus—the greatest friendship gift of all time! Jesus Christ was truly a gift we did not deserve, did nothing to receive, cannot repay, and will never fully understand until we meet Him in eternity. John 3:16 states, "For God so loved the world that He gave His only begotten Son, that whosoever believeth in Him shall not perish, but have everlasting life." God expressed His agape love towards us when He gave His only begotten Son, Jesus, to redeem our sins. This gift was loaded with benefits that cannot be earned—only received. In accepting Jesus as our Lord and Savior, we receive redemption, salvation, justification of sins, adoption into the Body of Christ, and the gift of eternal life. We also receive Jesus' peace, love, joy, and harmony as one, because of His graciousness towards us (John 14:27). He was God in the flesh and dwelt among us in love and fellowship, filled with grace and truth (John 1:14).

As beneficiaries and recipients of this most cherished gift from God, we can live a much more prosperous and stable life. We have assurances we never had before receiving the precious gift of salvation. We have hope we never knew and we have joy we cannot explain. All because we received the gift of life through Christ. Jesus said, "I came that you might have life and have it more abundantly" (John 10:10). Experiencing life through Christ means we live in a manner that is real and completely devoted to God. Living more abundantly means our lives exceed what is necessary for survival. Life will be superior and extravagant, more eminent, more remarkable, and more excellent! [4]

This all flows from accepting the gift of Jesus Christ. This life in abundance that He brings can also be experienced in our personal friendships. If He is at the center of our relationships our friendships can be real and active, harmonious and unified, exceeding anything we could ever have imagined. When God's Word governs our conduct in friendship, it is inevitable that we reap the benefits of God's intent. We will find ourselves loving and cherishing our friends as Jesus loves and cherishes us; thus, reaping the full benefits

---

[4] Libronix Digital Library System; Logos Bible Software. The King James Version. The Bible Knowledge Commentary, Passage Guide: John 10:10.

of Godly friendship. This is why Jesus commands us to love each other as He loved us (John 15:12).

God has blessed me with some very dear friends in ministry. I have experienced first-hand, the major differences in these friendships and those I encountered before I surrendered my heart to Christ and became obedient to His Word. An example of a particular friendship that comes to mind is my dear friend, Pastor Robyn. When I first met her, I never thought we would be friends. Pastor Robyn was assigned as my mentor in ministry but, I initially rejected her because I thought we had nothing in common. In my thinking that was grounds for dismissal!

We did not come from the same background, and I had no idea why I had been paired with her. I did not want to build a relationship because I didn't believe there was any benefit in it for me. I did not see her as a gift from God that should be cherished and valued. I used the same worldly, superficial criteria I spoke of earlier in this chapter. My mind had to be transformed before I could begin to develop an appreciation for her. I had to become a new person who was able to see life through the eyes of God. 2 Corinthians 5:17 states, "If any man be in Christ, he is a new creature: old things are passed away; behold, all things become new." As my thinking was renewed I began to mature. I began to see purpose and value I was unable to see before. Pastor Robyn and I began experiencing like-mindedness in terms of our desire to follow God's Word and embrace His plans for us. We formed a bond and trust that I never thought possible, and it continues to grow. This doesn't mean we always agree. But I've come to know it's because one of us—usually me—does not understand the application of the Scriptures properly. Once she helps me in this area and things are cleared up, we are fine.

This friendship is totally different from anything I experienced in my past. It is much more meaningful because it is based upon purpose and solidified by God's teachings, which we honor. Ephesians 4:2–3 defines my relationship with Pastor Robyn. "Be completely humble and gentle; be patient, bearing with one another in love. Make every effort to keep the unity of the Spirit through the bond of peace." Because we work very closely in ministry and realize God has blessed us with this gift of friendship, love, harmony and unity is our portion. The Holy Spirit empowers us to maintain the bond of peace because we have learned to cherish the relationship. Peace is our goal; reconciliation in all matters of difference is our aim. 2 Corinthians 5:18 states, "And all things are of God, who has reconciled us to Himself by Jesus Christ, and has given to us the ministry of reconciliation." We are to keep our friendships straight by reconciling our differences. This is what Jesus accomplished on the cross when He died so selflessly for our sins. His personal sacrifice reconciled us back to right relationship with God. In turn, we have been charged to reconcile our differences so we too can live in right relationship with each other. If we who profess Christ do not live according to His example, we will forfeit, as I ignorantly attempted to do, the very friendships that will be most beneficial to us.

The gift of friendship is to be cherished and protected so it can grow and flourish. This only happens when friendships are governed by God's standards. On the contrary, Satan's script for friendship involves everything pertaining to pleasing the flesh. Because the appetites of the flesh change so frequently, if our friendships follow his plan they cannot remain stable. The Apostle Paul aptly described the end result of following his pattern in relationships. Galatians 5:19–24 states:

Now the works of the flesh are these: adultery, fornication, uncleanness, lasciviousness, idolatry, witchcraft, hatred, variance, emulations, wrath, strife, seditions, heresies, envyings, murders, drunkenness, revellings, and such like: of which I have told you before, that those which do such things will not inherit the Kingdom of God. But the fruit of the Spirit is love, joy, peace, longsuffering, gentleness, goodness, faith, meekness, temperance: against such there is no law. Those that are Christ's have crucified the flesh with its affections and lusts.

As we see in this passage of Scriptures, following Satan's pattern of appeasing the flesh will lead to destructive, demonic behaviors that seek only to separate us from the love of God. However, when friendship is governed by the Word of God and we yield to the guidance of the Holy Spirit, we can expect the fruit of the Spirit to prevail in the relationship.

God created man for friendship with Him and with each other. He designed the order for friendships and relationships among us and gave Himself as the example to follow. That has not changed. No variables exist in Him. He gave us each other so we could forge meaningful, transparent relationships worthy of nurturing and care, which is what He originally wanted with Adam and Eve in the garden. The Bible says He came down from heaven to visit them "in the cool of the day" (Gen. 3:8) in the garden of Eden that He so graciously gave to them. God wanted to have fellowship with Adam and Eve. Unfortunately, instead of Adam and Eve embracing their intimacy with God, they allowed it to be broken at the vices of Satan. He convinced the pair to rebel against God so their harmony with Him and each other would be broken. He continues to do the same thing with us today. He constantly tries to entice us, as he did with Eve, with things we feel entitled to have. But, the good news is, nothing can negate God's original intentions for mankind. What God ordains will come to pass. He made certain to put the plan of redemption in place so we would not be eternally separated from Him and could regain sweet harmony and communion with Him. Fellowship with God is where joy in life and friendship comes from. In Psalm 16:11 the psalmist says to God, "You make to me the path of life; in Your presence is fullness of joy; and at Your right hand are pleasures forever more." Satan doesn't want us to have real, lasting joy with God. And, if we do not share this intimacy and love with God we do not have it to share with people. This is why Satan is determined to separate us from the presence of God. He knows very well that we will live miserable, self-serving lives incapable of experiencing the true love of God in all of our relationships.

God created us to *need* friendship and a sense of community that start with a relationship with Him. He has always promised to "walk among His people and be with them"(Lev. 26:12). There is a pattern of love and commitment from the Father to His people throughout the Old Testament. This same pattern continues into the New Testament. Jesus promised, "If anyone loves Me he will keep My Word; and My Father will love him, and We will come to him, and make Our abode with him" (John 14:23). Man was never meant to be absent from a relationship with God or people. That's why God created Eve from Adam's rib (Gen 2:22). "It is not good that man should be alone; I will make a help meet for him" (Gen. 2:18). Adam did not ask for her because he did not know he needed her; neither did he go looking for her. She was a gift from God. Check out the benefits:

In that passage, "God" is translated in Hebrew to *Elohim*. This name refers to God as the Supreme Creator who called man into existence (Gen. 1:27). *Elohim* also denotes God's position as magistrate, which means He is the Supreme Ruler in the affairs of man.[5] Only *Elohim* knows the purposes for which we were created and He holds the plan for how those purposes will be fulfilled on earth. Now, let's look at the word "good," which is translated in Hebrew to *towb*. This word means pleasant and agreeable; valuable in estimation and suitable; beneficial and prosperous. [6]Lastly, the phrase "help meet" means one who helps and succours. To succour means the person is able to assist and support in times of hardship and distress.[7] After studying God's character as *Elohim*, the Hebrew meaning of "good" and the phrase "help-meet," we can safely paraphrase Genesis 2:18 to mean, "It is not beneficial for any man to be alone. He needs a companion, partner, and co-laborer to accent his inadequacies; of which I (*Elohim*) alone am aware of. Only then will he be successful in executing My (*Elohim*) purposes on the earth." As we learn from this example, God gifts us with friends and spouses to walk alongside us to support our divine purpose. Just as Eve was given to Adam, we too have been given friends and loved ones who should be regarded as good and perfect gifts from our Almighty God!

---

[5]   www.blueletterbible.org. "Elohim." Strong's Concordance, Hebrews 430. Genesis 1:27.

[6]   www.blueletterbible.org. "Good." Strong's Concordance, Hebrews 2896. Genesis 2:18.

[7]   www.lexico.com. "Help Meet." Oxford Dictionary. 2020.

Chapter One Discussion Questions

1. This chapter focused on friends being gifts from God. Before reading this, where did you think they came from?

2. What is meant by God's gifts being good and perfect. Does that change how you will view friendships going forward?

3. Has God given you a "help meet"? Discuss how their presence has impacted your life. If you answered no, what will your expectations of this person be when they come?

4. How do you select your friends? What has influenced your choices?

5. After reading this chapter, are you beginning to think of your friendships in a different way?

Chapter Two

—·····+·+·=·=·+·=·+·◇·=·+·=·=·+·+·····—

How Does Jesus Define Friends?

"This is My commandment, that ye love one another, as I have loved you. Greater love hath no man than this, that he lay down his life for his friends. Ye are my friends, if you do whatsoever I command you" (John 15:12–14).

The word "friend" is a broad term because it's often used to describe a variety of relationships. Some people use "friend" to describe people they have deep connections with and people they may feel strong loyalty toward. They believe these friends will be with them for life, through thick and thin. Other people may use "friend" when referring to casual acquaintances or people they share common interests with. These types of friendships may be forged in the workplace, at school or church, or other places. The Barna Group conducted a study that suggests that no matter where friends meet, people tend to be drawn to individuals who are most like them. In the study, when asked whether their current friends are mostly similar to themselves or different in a number of areas, the majority of those consulted always chose mostly similar. This was true for religious beliefs (sixty-two percent said "similar"), race or ethnicity (seventy-four percent said "similar"), income (fifty-six percent said "similar"),education level (sixty-three percent said "similar"), social status (seventy percent said "similar"), political views (sixty-two percent said "similar"),and life stages (sixty-nine percent said "similar").[8] While similar interests are common factors in many friendships, still others forge friendships with people who have done favors for them or have looked out for them. These relationships may offer a sense of support and loyalty; feelings that these friends will serve as an anchor in difficult situations.

Not only does our reference to friends refer to several reasons for the connections, but, as we will learn in this study, there are many purposes and structures for friendships. Some are short term and may not be intended to have longevity. Others are long term and intended to weather the seasons and storms of life. Some develop instantly, as if it were always meant to be. While others are transitional in nature and develop over a period of time. These relationships are often never actualized because many people do not invest the time it takes to nurture them. Still some friendships may cause intense friction and discomfort, requiring a great deal of work and commitment. While other relationships come with great ease and satisfaction. Regardless of the nature of the friendship, we all have them. We all yearn for them and we all truly need them. These relationships are necessary in our lives because we were born to need fellowship, which is more than just having company. Our souls yearn for friendships because we are wired that way. This is the reason many of us live miserably in the absence

---

[8] The Barna Group; *U.S. Adults Have Few Friends.* Articles in Culture and Media; October 23, 2018.

of them. Due to the challenges friendships can bring, many people reject the very notion of them despite the fact that we were all born to need them. Friendships are as critical as food and water. This is also the reason many of us force people into our lives. Our desperation for friends causes us to hoard them. The reason these deranged beliefs about friendships exist is because the human heart and mind has been contaminated by Satan. Because of the fall in the garden, we are all born into sin and possess a sin nature. Until we are cleansed by the blood of Jesus and transformed in our thinking, our understanding of the acquisition, purpose, and value of friendships, and everything else for that matter, is most definitely off (Rom. 12:1–2).

The only way to determine God's true intent for friendship requires an examination of how our Lord used the term throughout Scripture. What patterns can we see from the Old to the New Testaments? Are there variations in meaning from one passage to another? If they differ in meaning, what are the consistent nuggets we are to glean from the combined definitions? Let's continue our examination and see what we can ascertain.

I came across this great article on friends and friendship on the internet by Carl B. Bridges, Jr. He did an outstanding job breaking down the various meanings of the word "friend" and "friendship" in the Bible. Bridges concluded that the idea of friends and friendship involve three components: association, loyalty, and affection. There are also three levels of meaning: friendship as association only, friendship as association plus loyalty, and friendship as association, plus loyalty, plus affection. [9]

---

[9]   Biblestudytools.com/dictionaries/bakers-evangelical-dictionary/ friend-friendship.html; Friend / Friendship. Carl B. Bridges, Jr. Copyright 1996.

According to *Nelson's Illustrated Dictionary of the Bible*, the term "friend" commonly refers to a person someone loves and trusts; a close companion or comrade. One of the earliest uses of the term "friend" is when God spoke to Moses. Exodus 33:11 states, "Face to face as a man speaks to his friend." The Hebrew definition for friend in that passage means fellow citizen, neighbor, or intimate companion. So, Exodus 33:11 is saying that God spoke to Moses clearly and openly, as with a companion. "Face to face" is a figurative expression also suggesting openness and friendship. This reminds me of when Jesus told His disciples in John 15:15, "I no longer call you servants, I now call you friends because all things I have heard from My Father, I have made known unto you." This suggests a level of transparency in friendships.

The New Testament uses several Greek words for "friend," including *philos*, which is a term of endearment when referring to someone dearly loved (James 2:23). *Hetairos* means companion or comrade. (Matt. 20:13; 22:12; 26:50). Last, *plesion* means neighbor. The New Testament also uses a variety of kinship terms, such as brother and sister, that extend outside the biological family to note feelings of significance and special affection (Matt. 12:50). For the purpose of this study, let us focus specifically on what Jesus meant when He said, "This is My commandment, that ye love one another, as I have loved you. Greater love hath no man than this, that he lay down his life for his friends. Ye are my friends, if you do whatsoever I command you" (John 15:12-14). Let's look at the context in which Jesus spoke these powerful words from the Gospel of John.

Jesus was teaching His final discourse to His disciples and had already made His triumphal entry into Jerusalem (John 12:12-19). Jesus had washed the disciple's feet John

13:1-15). He has foretold of His betrayal (John 13:21-30). He has assured them He is going to prepare a place for them and will come back again (John 14:1-3). He comforts them by letting them know they will never be alone and in His physical absence, they are to be assured the Holy Ghost will come (John 14:16-18; 26).

After Jesus assures His disciples of these things, He draws His attention to His eternal, intimate relationship with them. He described Himself as the True Vine, which means He is the full embodiment of what they should become (John 15:1-2).The disciples should faithfully execute the ministry of reconciliation as God's representatives on earth. The only way to do that was to be faithful to all they had been taught. They had to remain loyal to Jesus' doctrine just as He had been loyal to God (John 7:16).

Jesus described His disciples as branches and Himself as the Vine, their source. If they did not abide in Him, they wouldn't be able to reproduce disciples. They would be useless to His ministry. This is why the parable says, "the man that abides not in Him will dry up, become withered and be burned" (John 15:6). He issued a primary command to love each other as He had loved them with the same love that He experienced with His Father. That wasn't just any kind of love. This was *agape* love, which is one of four words used for "love" in Greek. The other three words are *phileo*, *storge*, and *eros*. Understanding the different meanings of these terms is necessary because the clarity will unveil the deception that all love is the same and should be given to people in a like manner. This understanding will also reveal a deeper value of how Jesus defines friends and His expectations for the relationship. Each Greek word for "love" is defined below.

Phileo love speaks of brotherly love and love based upon common interests (Matt. 10:37; John 5:20). The city of Philadelphia is known as the city of brotherly love because *phileo* is the root word. Brotherly love is most often found between really close friends, such as Jonathan and David. Both individuals seek to please and make the other happy. We do not extend this type of love toward enemies.

Storge love refers to naturally occurring, familial love, such as between a mother and child or brother and sister. While *storge* is not directly used in the New Testament, the opposite form of the word is, which is *astorgos* in Greek. *Astorgos* means "no love." It is devoid of natural and instinctive affection toward kindred. An example of the use of *astorgos* is when sinful humanity is described as having "no understanding, no fidelity, no mercy, and no love" (Romans 1:31). The Apostle Paul also used describes *astorgos* in 2 Timothy 3:3, which translates to "without love."

Eros describes passionate or affectionate love. In English, *eros* translates to "erotic." This is the type of love many of us build our marriages on. While passion and affection are necessary in marriage, this love cannot solely sustain the relationship. Ask yourself two questions:

1. What happens to the marriage when the fire goes out?

2. What holds it together past sexual attraction and passion?

Agape love is the most powerful, noble type of love because it is self-sacrificial. It involves faithfulness, commitment, and an act of personal will that extends far beyond feelings and emotions. If someone shows you *agape* love, it means they love you past passion and affection. He or she loves despite circumstances and is reliable and continuous. *Agape* love is described beautifully in 1 Corinthians 13: 1-13. This is the type of love God commands us to have toward each other and even our enemies because *agape* love causes us to see people through His eyes.

I loved my husband when he asked me to marry him. I was attracted to him, but I didn't know if mere attraction and admiration could sustain us throughout time. I knew God's divine intervention and guidance was needed. So, when I said "Yes," it was only after I consulted the Lord in prayer and asked Him, "Help me to love him like You love him, and help me to always see him like You see him." From that day on, God answered my prayer. I didn't know much then, but I knew enough to realize *eros* love would not sustain us forever. I needed God to teach me how to love my husband with *agape* love and He did. God has empowered me for twenty-six years to love sacrificially, constantly giving of myself through our differences and my own self-serving purposes. I have mastered loving past my preferences, even when my flesh disagrees.

Agape love is missing in many friendships and marriages because there is no ability to love like this without Jesus.

The world cannot know what agape love is because it is of God. Apart from an intimate relationship with God, this love is not possible.(1 John 2:15; 4:7-8). Satan painted a false picture of what it means to love. This deception is endlessly cast and displayed in every area of our lives. You cannot turn the television on without witnessing the sexual exploitation of men and women, of which many people sadly think is the way love is supposed to be. Some people find themselves trapped in these fruitless relationships because they were conned by Satan. The bottom line is this, relationships that function according to standards of the world are only about things that please the eyes and flesh (1 John 2:15-16). That's why many relationships easily end when the flesh is no longer satisfied. Those relationships have nothing to do with the purpose and security of eternal life. Relationships established according to the standards of this world in no way reflect what Jesus meant when He challenged His disciples to love each other as He loved them. As a matter of fact, what is believed to be love in worldly relationships is a total opposite of Jesus' command to exhibit agape love. This false impression of love is orchestrated by Satan who has complete influence over worldly thinking. He is the father of lies and his goal is always to deceive and separate people from the true love of God (John 8:44). His patterns of these attempts at separating God's people are seen throughout the Bible. Starting with Eve in the Garden, to the disciple Peter, Satan desires to trick God's people into thinking his ways are the right ways, but they clearly lead only to destruction. God does not want our friendships to end in destruction. He wants them to grow and flourish to heights that exceed our wildest imaginations! The only way these heights can be realized is if we exhibit God's agape love one to another. Without it there is no basis for Godly friendship.

As we explore John 15:13-14, let's determine who Jesus referred to as friends, and what the requirements were for those relationships. The word friend used in these verses is the Greek word *philos*. In its root is the term *phileo* which refers to brotherly love. As we now see, Jesus does not separate the terms love and friend. They are often used interchangeably by Him in Scripture. Therefore, we will explore this term for friends, *phileo,* as we determine the practical application of this study to our lives.

Here's the scene in John 15:1-17: Jesus was on His way to Calvary. This scene took place in an intimate, personal setting with His disciples. This was Jesus' final discourse or lessons to them. At this point, Jesus' disciples had become His companions. He had developed a brotherly relationship with each of them, despite their differences, inadequacies, and uniqueness. This relationship would extend throughout eternity, and they would forever be with Him (John 3:16; John 10:28; 1 John 5:11–13).

Jesus' bond with His disciples had a common denominator—their obedience to the Father. One example of this is when Jesus taught in the synagogue and was interrupted by Mary and Joseph (Matt. 12:46–50, Mark 3:31-35, Luke 8:19–21). This is an important teaching because Jesus revealed the essence of brotherhood and family. During His teaching, Jesus was informed that His family was outside and wanted to speak to Him. In the Hebrew culture, family was everything. In front of His Jewish audience, Jesus audibly asks a question, "Who is My mother? And who are My brethren (Matthew 12:48)? Jesus knew the answer to this question, but He seized the opportunity to lay the groundwork for teaching a kingdom principle to His audience.

Jesus answered His own question by stretching forth His hands toward His disciples and saying, "Behold My mother and My brethren" (Matthew 12:49). He told the audience that "His disciples were His family!" Then Jesus reinforced why He said it: "For whosoever shall do the will of My Father which is in heaven, the same is My brother, and sister, and mother" (Matthew 12:50).

The word "brother" refers to an intimate friend, a fellow follower of God, united to each other by the bond of affection. This is a kinship term that extended beyond the boundaries of the biological family. In addition to the relationship,

23

the inherent meaning of Jesus' profound declaration to this audience is that true discipleship and friendship with Jesus comes only through obedience to His Father's Word. This was further reiterated in the next verse when Jesus identified the requirement to be His friend, "Ye are my friends, if you do whatsoever I command you" (John 15:14).

Let's remember this is Jesus' final opportunity to teach His disciples before He proceeded to Calvary. At such a critical time in His ministry, why would He pause to teach about friendship? I believe it was because He knew His death at Calvary would show His disciples the greatest example of *agape* love towards friends ever known. Jesus' example of humility, courage, faithfulness, and devotion was what the disciples were to replicate among themselves for the remainder of their earthly lives. They were to support each other through persecution and death, trials and tribulations. If they were not willing to commit to each other as true brothers in Christ and extend *agape* love, operating in full obedience to the Father, they would not make it. Thus, He commanded His disciples to embrace the highest level of love in friendship, just the way He had loved them (John 15:12). *Agape* style!

In closing this chapter, I pray we will forever keep Jesus' definition of "friend" towards His disciples before us. He referred to them as friends because He viewed them as His brothers and companions. He formed a kinship with them that centered around their obedience to the Father and the agape love which only comes from the Father (1 John 4:7-9). Jesus extended this love to them, and we are to extend it to each other. Without this love, our relationships constitute nothing more than a façade and false image of true, godly friendship.

Chapter Two Discussion Questions

1. Up to this point, what or who has shaped your thinking regarding friendships?

2. Do you believe you have extended agape love to your friends?

3. Did you believe all love was the same and should be given to everyone in like manner?

4. In your own words, write down the definition of a real friend as you understand it after reading this chapter.

5. How does what you wrote differ from your previous understanding of friendship?

6. Examine your requirements for friendship. Do they follow Jesus' criteria as seen in Matthew 12:50 and John 15:14?

7. Will you establish an action plan to unravel the impact worldly thinking may have had on your friendships?

Chapter Three

The Seasonal Nature of Some Friendships

"To everything there is a time and a season, and a time to every purpose under heaven" (Ecclesiastes 3:1).

The concept of seasonal events in our lives can be confusing. Typically, we approach life from a place of seeking what we want exactly when we want it. We are often impatient and unwilling to wait for anything. King Solomon shared truth to help us better understand the varying purposes of events and people in our lives, and why it is so critical for us to be mindful of God's strategic timing. The word "season" in Hebrew is defined as a "set time" or an "appointed time." King Solomon taught us that seasons indicate a duration of time that has been appointed by God for all things. Friendships and relationships are not exempt.

Have you ever had a close friend in one season of your life, but as you got older you felt you had nothing in common anymore? If you parted ways from that friend, do you ever feel guilty that you left? If that friend parted ways with you, do you feel abandoned? These are common scenarios. After examining numerous stories in the Bible, I reached a conclusion that these changing friendships are part of Christian life. As God sanctifies us and we change, our priorities and passions, thoughts and conduct, friendships and relationships will also change. We will no longer find interests in many of the things that once intrigued us. For numerous reasons, many of which we will look at in this chapter, some of us are determined to hold onto outdated relationships and drag people into new seasons of our lives when they may not belong. That is because many of us share an understanding and commitment to friendships that is based upon history, not purpose.

We believe history with people means we can share the same comradery, values, and interests for the rest of our lives. Often when we force those continued relationships, and suddenly an old friend cannot provide the support we've grown to need, we become frustrated. But it is not their fault. Many of our former friends are simply no longer aligned with God's plan and direction for us. This does not mean those friends no longer have any purpose in our lives. However, while they may have had a major purpose at one point, their impact in the new season may be reduced. It will be difficult to look to those friends to fulfill new areas of need because they simply do not understand them. Our once similar values are not the same anymore and our allegiances have changed. Unfortunately, many of us do not have the courage to embrace these changes so we insist upon uniting history in friendship with our newly revealed Godly purpose. This is very common in two areas of life: friendships we maintained for many years and relatives within the family structure.

Have you ever wondered why family reunions with siblings, cousins, and close family friends can become toxic? Why is it that after the novelty of seeing one another wears off, the fighting and arguing begins? There could be a plethora of reasons for this, but there are several theories to consider. One theory is that people are no longer close. Someone may have grown in ways others are totally unfamiliar with. So, when remarks are made or behaviors are examined that were once perceived as okay, tension rises. The second theory is that families and old friends tend to believe relationships should always remain the same. That is not realistic though and no one should want to remain at status quo. We were created to grow in every aspect of life. In fact, as Christians, we are commanded to grow. Paul said, "Be not conformed to this world, but be ye transformed by the renewing of your mind, that ye may prove what is that good, and acceptable and perfect will of God for your lives" (Rom. 12:1–2). Christians must be transformed back into the image of Christ not stuck on remaining the same people they were before Christ entered their lives (Eph. 4:14–15). Old friends and family members who have not experienced salvation are clueless of the impact the Lord, His Word, and the Holy Spirit can have on a person's life. As a result, friends and family may disregard your salvation. They may behave as if certain behaviors such as cursing, drinking, gossiping, and other habits are still acceptable. This friction can cause tremendous stress for Christians.

I completed a study on the spirit of familiarity, which is a damnable spirit because of the many destructive acts it sets out to do. One such destructive act is to stunt an individual's growth so he or she disregards new seasons of life. Using the story found in Matthew 13:53–58, I studied the people who observed Jesus during His childhood in Nazareth and how they attempted to impose the spirit of familiarity upon Him. In one example, Jesus, as an adult, went home and taught in one of the local synagogues. People knew Jesus, but only as a little boy since He had grown up there. Jesus' teaching was amazing and He astonished everyone. Instead of embracing His obvious anointing, the crowd questioned the source of His wisdom and ability to perform the mighty works they witnessed. They did not understand the season Jesus was in. His ministry was in full motion and He was fulfilling His purpose.

Jesus' familial ties were all the crowd knew. They questioned the origin of His gifts (Matt 13:56). The Bible says the crowds became offended by Jesus, which means they became indignant (Matt 13:57). They disapproved because they were unfamiliar with His anointing. Jesus responded, "A prophet is without honor in His own country and in His own house" (Matt 13:57). As a result, Jesus did not do many works in Nazareth because of their disbelief. Jesus' hometown people missed out on healing, teaching, and deliverance (Matt 13:58).

The spirit of familiarity is often present in families because family members can attempt to hold loved ones in the same season they were in when they had a close relationship. The person who experiences spiritual growth is not the person they knew. This is why family members and old friends take great pride in referring to times past when they were different than the present. It makes them feel comfortable because that's the person they once knew.

Some of us insist on engaging in toxic gatherings with our families and friends because we want to attempt to maintain a right relationship with them. However, a right relationship with each other is not possible when you are not in the right relationship with God. If your family or friends never know God for themselves, they will disregard your new life and season in Christ. If this is the case, rather than fellowship, we should be looking for evangelistic opportunities to bring those people closer to God.

Now that we have exposed the unhealthy nature of some of these forced, out of season relationships based entirely upon history, let us continue this conversation by looking at the potential damage that can be caused when we drag people into seasons of which they do not belong.

Let's begin this section by reviewing Abraham's choice to take his nephew, Lot, into a new season of his life. Genesis 12:1–2 states, "Get out of your country, and from your kindred, and from your father's house, and go to a land that I will show you. And I will make a great nation out of you, and I will bless you, and make your name great; and you will be a blessing."

The short of Abraham's life is: Abram, Abraham's original name, became the first patriarch of the Hebrew nation. His father, Terah, had a brother named Haran. Haran was Lot's father.

Haran was also the name of the city where Terah moved his family (Gen 11:31).[10] That background is important when it comes to understanding why God called Abram away from his family. Haran was a trading center in northern Aram, the land known today as Syria. It was situated on one of the main trade routes between Babylonia and the Mediterranean Sea. All kinds of people were in and out of the ports, which attracted the worship of false gods and idolatry. Haran's citizens worshipped Sin, the moon god, which translates to the "lord of wisdom" and "father of the gods."

---

[10] Nelson's Illustrated Dictionary of the Bible; "Terah." Herbert Lockyer, Sr. Editor, Thomas Nelson Publishers, Copyright 1986. p.459.

[11] One of the moon god's titles was "lord of the Diadem." His chief attribute was wisdom, which he supposedly dispensed to humans and the gods who regularly visited him. Because idolatry was so prevalent in Abram's hometown and within his family, God had to separate him in order to fulfill His purpose.

God will always separate those He has called from influences He knows yield ungodly outcomes. He usually calls us independent of anyone else, for every disciple must bear his/her cross alone (Luke 14:27). God is not going to call us to a great work and leave us surrounded by false gods and idol worship. This separation and splitting can be painful because it calls for major life adjustments. We may encounter criticism, insults, and a number of other reactions because our former close friends and family simply do not understand what is happening in our lives. While our concerns in these seasons will inevitably be drawn to what these transitions may look like in the eyes of our family and friends, God is looking at purpose. So, Abram departed as the Lord had commanded, and he took his nephew, Lot. Abram was seventy-five years old when he received this order from God (Gen 12:5).

How do you think your friends and families wouldrespond if you, at seventy-five said, "God spoke to me and told me to leave all of you and go to a foreign land I know nothing about. He requires only that I trust Him for He has promised to make me the father of a great nation that is large in number and significant in purpose." If you are truthful, most of them would think you had lost your mind!

---

[11] Nelson's Illustrated Dictionary of the Bible; "Sin-moon-god." Herbert Lockyer, Sr. Editor, Thomas Nelson Publishers, Copyright 1986. p.459.

The Bible does not tell us that Abram consulted his friends and family before he obeyed God's command. Many of us abort our calling because we consult people who know nothing about our call, have no insight into what it means, and only have their personal interests at heart.

I remember when the Lord told me to leave my first teaching job and go to Bowling Green, Ohio for graduate school. Everyone asked me: Why are you going so far? Where is this place? You should not leave your great job! I went to Bowling Green despite everyone's opinions. Those people weren't trying to steer me wrong, they just did not know what God was doing in my life. God put me on His path by sending me to Bowling Green. Furthermore, I had been drifting into behaviors that would have compromised God's long-term purposes for my life. My friends and family didn't see me becoming a pastor or serving as the vice president of a great Bible college and theological seminary.

Like Abram, there will be times in our lives when God will force us to follow Him into new seasons with little or no information. He may command us to walk that path without friends or family for a season. Going solo with God is common among His chosen ones which is why we often insist upon bringing friendships and loved ones into seasons they are not meant to be in.

Such was the case of Abram taking Lot with him. Abram was a man of great substance. He was rich in silver, gold, and cattle (Gen 13:2). Lot was wealthy also and had many flocks and herds. God made their substance so great that they would not be able to dwell together in the same land (Gen 13:6). God also allowed strife to develop between Abram's herdsmen and Lot's (Gen 13:7). This ultimately caused Abram to end the strife by parting ways with Lot (Gen 13:9). This was God's way of separating Abram from Lot because

He knew Abram would not want strife to prevail between them. God knew Abram's heart and that the bond he shared with Lot was something he cherished and wanted to preserve. In Abram's case, the only way to preserve the relationship was to separate from it. This is also true in many of our situations. We often find that once we leave the relationship to follow God, He will restore it in another season; ultimately, preserving the bonds of friendship. Because this is not always the case, a key requirement in our relationship with God is putting Him first and trusting Him for the people we need along the journey (Matt 10:37).

Upon separating from Abram, Lot made a choice to live in a heathenistic environment among people who were wicked and sinners before the Lord in excess (Gen 13:12-13). In that season of Lot's life, God continued to use Abram to rescue and preserve Lot time and time again from the destruction that surrounded him (Gen 14:12-16). I'm certain Abram did not take Lot's ungodly choices into account when he began his journey with God. Abram was counted as a righteous man, but he ended up with the burden of caring for an irresponsible, ungrateful loved one who proved to be more of a burden than a benefit. It was Abram's choice to bring Lot with him not God's command. Like Abram, we all have to live with the consequences of our choices. That is why we should consult trusted biblical counsel before making important decisions. Proverbs 11:14 states, "Where no counsel is the people fall; but there is safety in the multitude of counsel."

Let's look at another seasonal relationship example: the virgin Mary and her cousin, Elisabeth.

This story is found in Luke 1:26-38. The virgin Mary was visited by the angel Gabriel and informed she would conceive a son and call Him Jesus. He would be great and reign over the house of Jacob forever (Luke 1:31-33). As anyone would be, Mary was confused and perplexed. Mary asked Gabriel, "How can this be seeing as how I have never been with a man" (Luke 1:34)? Gabriel assured Mary that she would be impregnated by the Holy Ghost and she would give birth to the Son of God. The angel also told Mary that her cousin, Elisabeth, had conceived a baby in old age by the supernatural power of God (Luke 1:36-37). Upon receiving this information, Mary resolved, "Be it unto me according to thy word" (Luke 1:38).

Can you imagine being visited by an angel of God and receiving this awesome assignment?

When we observe Mary in this story, we note she didn't consult anyone but Elisabeth. The Scriptures do not tell us she consulted her mother, siblings or friends. The only other person the passage mentions is her husband to be, Joseph; that's it. It's important we note that Joseph was a Hebrew man, knowledgeable of Scriptures, and governed according to the laws of the Hebrew nation. One of the laws of the nation was that a woman would be stoned if caught in the act of adultery (Lev. 20:10, Deut. 22:22, John 8:1–11). Because of this, Mary must have been fearful that Joseph would have her publicly stoned as a result of her inexplicable pregnancy. But she did not need to worry, God already had a plan to take care of Joseph.

There are two very important lessons to observe in this story. The first is: When God calls us to follow Him He will take care of all details of significance in our lives. In Mary's case, of grave concern in her life would have been Joseph. Thus, God sent an angel to Joseph who told him Mary's child was conceived by the Holy Ghost and that he should not fear taking her as his wife. The angel also told Joseph that the child would be named Jesus and He would save people from their sins (Matt 1:18-24). Joseph needed this assurance so he would know the prophecies of old spoken by Isaiah, were being fulfilled though Mary. "A virgin would conceive and bring forth Emmanuel, whose name means God with us" (Isa. 7:14). As a result, Joseph was convinced the pregnancy was of God, did as the angel said, and took Mary to be his wife (Matt 1:24).

The second lesson we glean from Mary's story is that we should listen to every word God says and know that nothing is irrelevant. The Bible does not tell us that Gabriel instructed Mary to go to Elisabeth. However, Gabriel mentioned Elisabeth because she conceived a child under supernatural, miraculous conditions. She did not take anyone with her, but the Bible says Mary went to Elisabeth quickly (Luke 1:39). As soon as Elisabeth heard Mary's voice, her baby leaped in her womb and she was filled with the Holy Ghost (Luke 1:41). Elisabeth loudly called to Mary and blessed and pronounced blessing on the fruit of her womb. Elisabeth acknowledged Mary's blessings as a result of believing the angel of the Lord and made it known there would be a performance of those things she had heard (Luke 1:39–45).

God placed Elisabeth in that season of Mary's life because she would be able to give Mary the spiritual assurance and counsel she needed to move forward in her assignment. God filled Elisabeth with the Holy Ghost so she could speak as His oracle. The two shared God's hand on their lives and were connected in purpose. The Bible says Mary stayed with Elisabeth for three months (Luke 1:56). This story proves the power and impact the right seasonal friendship can have.

I am reminded of a critical juncture in my life. My first role as Superintendent of Schools came as a result of a horrific situation in my school district. My former boss, then serving as the Superintendent, was arrested for sodomizing a child. Everyone was seeking direction and what to do in order to move forward. That night, my board of directors appointed me as the Acting Superintendent. By the time I returned to work the next day, I entered a building swarming with police detectives and newspaper reporters. Employees were crying and seeking direction. We were all devastated, confused, and completely uncertain of how to break this news to the community and how to proceed. I did not know what was going on nor what to expect in this new role as Acting Superintendent.

The only thing I knew was to get in touch with my Pastor. It was the first time I had ever called her because I had only been at the church a few months. Fortunately, we were able to connect. The first thing she said to me was, "Trish, calm down and let's pray." She prayed for me and settled me in that moment. She gave me counsel and encouragement in a time I desperately needed it, and she walked me through this tumultuous season every day of it for over 14 months! From that point on, she has spoken into my life. I can't imagine the counsel I would have received if I had chosen to contact an old friend who didn't know where I was on my spiritual journey. While I truly wanted to share my fear and pain with them, I needed a divinely appointed person from God and one I knew I could trust and rely on. My Bishop was my Elisabeth. Thankfully for me, her assignment was not for three months, but is for life!

We often get entangled in friendships and relationships because of our history and sense of loyalty; but when you're an agent of the Lord, we must first determine our purpose, which will ultimately determine our friends. We have to trust God and seek His counsel on these matters, knowing He will order relationships as they should be and we will all benefit as a result (Matt. 6:33; Pro 3:5-6). Regardless of who is uncomfortable and may not agree with those who are chosen to accompany us on our path, we must know with full assurance, it is the will of God for our lives. He is intentional about who He wants in our ears and at what points in life He wants them there. Some friends may be permanent, but most assuredly, others will play their key roles in seasons.

Chapter Three Discussion Questions

1. Identify areas of your personal growth that have been compromised as a result of acquiescing to the spirit of familiarity.

2. Going forward, how will you assess who belongs and does not belong in your life at varying seasons?

3. Consider whether your current friendships exist because of history or purpose. How do you assess the benefits and/or disadvantages of both?

4. Are you being criticized and maybe even ostracized for leaving, at God's command? After studying Abram's life, how will you deal with this in the future?

5. Many of us attempt to hold on to friendships when we know their season is over. Are you insisting on holding on to dead friendships for fear of standing alone?

6. How will you avoid the unnecessary stress caused when God gives direction others may deem as crazy and impossible?

7. Consider the friends who feed your soul in this season of your life. Who are you in a purposeful fellowship with?

Chapter Four

The Instant Bonding in Some Friendships

"And it came to pass, when he had made an end of speaking unto Saul, that the soul of Jonathan was knit with the soul of David, and Jonathan loved him as his own soul. And Saul took him that day, and would let him go no more home to his father's house. Then Jonathan and David made a covenant, because he loved him as his own soul" (1 Sam. 18:1–3).

I met my friend Kanyere in an airport while traveling to the same destination. Kanyere was traveling with her mother and aunt. Immediately, I felt as if I'd always known her. We spoke like old friends who were reunited. We hugged and laughed.

Before I go any further with this story, I have to share a twist so you can fully understand the story. I have an identical twin, Bishop Julia McMillan. She and her husband are pastors in Tampa, Florida. My sister was hosting a women's conference that year. Kanyere and I were both working at the conference. Julia had known Kanyere for years, so she told me about her beforehand. So, when we made eye contact in the airport, our meeting was inevitable. Shortly after our salutations and breakfast, Kanyere and I spoke as if we had been friends for years. It wasn't long before we began discussing the Word of God, the need for the teaching and preaching of His Word, and how to develop those called to ministry work. As our conversation continued, I already began to see why our connection had to take place.

Kanyere was a young pastor. She was grappling with some training matters, infrastructure development, and other issues with the vocation. Kanyere was also a distant disciple of my Bishop McCullough for years. Bishop McCullough had spoken into Kanyere's life at critical junctures on her journey. Kanyere had even attended our church for a season.

God had planted seeds over the years to lead up to our connection in the airport. As Kanyere spoke, I heard my spirit say, "She needs us. She needs Beth Rapha. She has no idea that all the things she's expressing need for are at her fingertips. If she comes into my life, she is going to come into my spiritual family's life, including Bishop McCullough and other key figures in the ministry." I knew God sent Kanyere to me so she could receive the help she needed in that season of her ministry. As the weekend progressed, I had the opportunity to hear Kanyere preach. She handled God's Word with such care. Her theology was on point and her scholarship was beyond reproach. Then I witnessed her in prayer. As Kanyere clutched her mother's and aunt's hands, crying out to the Father for their family, I knew her prayers were sincere. I could not wait to get back to New York and share my experience with my Pastor.

Kanyere is still in our lives today, but there's more to this divine union. I later found out that Kanyere had been praying for true friends. She asked the Lord to send her a friend who would share in her love for Him, someone who would be able to edify her and counsel her in the ways of God as she walked her journey, and one who would walk it out with her. Kanyere will tell you that wasn't an offense to the friends she already had. She desired a new friend for a different purpose and God answered her prayer. He didn't just send her one friend, He sent her two who happened to be identical twins. Kanyere and I are friends and covenant partners in the Gospel of Jesus Christ and it is wonderful. Our friendship is God ordained and an example of being knitted because of purpose.

This is my personal example of the instantaneous nature of friendships. There are many more I could share, but now we will dive into the much talked about biblical friendship of Jonathan and David. Their friendship is one of the most coveted, misunderstood friendships in the Bible. It is coveted because of the obvious love, bond, and faithfulness of both David and Jonathan—something many of us miss in our friendships. Their relationship is misunderstood because the world does not understand the agape love of God that binds people together in purpose. Thus, this friendship has been grossly mischaracterized and is often used to validate homosexuality and other perverted forms of relationships.

Several passages of the Bible strongly denounce homosexuality (Gen. 1:26–27, Lev. 18:22, Lev. 20:13, Rom. 1:18–25). Because the Bible does not contradict itself, concluding that David and Jonathan were in a homosexual relationship is wrong. Their relationship came about strictly because of purpose and was ordained by God at the precise time it needed to happen. The love David and Jonathan shared was not *eros* love. The Hebrew term for love in 1 Samuel 18:1 is *ahav*, which has several meanings, but as it pertains to David and Jonathan it means to have close ties of friendship. In a political sense, *ahav* means loyalty. *Ahav* can reflect sexual love, but only within the context of God's laws for marriage. Since homosexuality does not honor God's laws for marriage, it cannot be used to justify marriage of the same sex. Because it is so common for our preferences for mates to be based upon physical attraction and erotic tendencies, it is also common that anything other than this type of attraction would be viewed as abnormal and perverted. Scriptures mention twice that Jonathan loved David as much as he loved his own soul. This means he loved and cared for David as much as he cared for himself (1 Sam. 18:1). This love Jonathan had for David is the same love Jesus taught His disciples to extend to each other. We are commanded to "Love thy neighbor as thyself" (Matt. 22:35–40, Mark 12:31).

Let's look at David and Jonathan's backgrounds before they met. This helps to better understand why God ordered this divine connection. Jonathan was the oldest son of King Saul and the rightful heir to the throne. David was the youngest son of Jesse of Bethlehem. Both sons were warriors and shared a strong faith in God. David volunteered to take down Goliath, the giant who defied the Lord's armies (1 Sam 17:26). Upon defeating Goliath, David found himself in King Saul's presence once again. Previously, David played the harp for King Saul and served as his armor bearer (1 Sam 16:21-23). Following the defeat of Goliath, David met Jonathan. Scripture says their souls were instantly knitted and they entered into a covenant relationship. This means upon meeting they immediately established an alliance of friendship and obligation of support.

Shortly after that, Saul became very envious of and angry with David because his defeat was more celebrated than his own. The king felt his glory diminish and blamed David. Saul watched David from that point on with the intent to kill him for stealing his glory (1 Sam 18:1–9).

Jonathan learned Saul wanted to kill David. In a weak attempt to manipulate Jonathan, Saul told his son that as long as David lived, he would never inherit the throne as King of Israel (1 Sam 20:31). Here's a great lesson: When we allow our friends or family to impose rebellious ways on us, they have crossed a boundary. Saul had no right to try and manipulate Jonathan.

Exodus 10:12 commands us to honor our mother and our father, but we have to know that the word "honor" means we are to love, cherish, and respect our parents. It does not mean we must follow them in their ungodly ways. Saul fell prey to the spirits of jealousy and entitlement. He lived his days suspicious of David and fearing that he wanted all he had acquired, including Jonathan's love and faithfulness. Saul built his life around his own self-preservation. He thought only of himself which caused him to become irrational and depressed, which is how he ended his life (1 Sam. 31:1–6).

On the other hand, it did not intimidate Jonathan that David had been anointed to be king by God and it did not affect Jonathan's righteous decision to support David. Unlike his father King Saul, upon meeting David, Jonathan acquiesced his kingship in reverence and honor of God's divine election of David to be king.[12] While Saul was enraged at the very thought of someone else stealing his glory, his

---

[12] Libronix Digital Library System; Logos Bible Software. The King James Version. The Bible Knowledge Commentary, Passage Guide:1 Samuel 18.

son Jonathan graciously bowed to God's choice and humbly acquiesced his right to the throne. David and Jonathan never experienced rivalry between them. Because they were men of great faith and they loved and honored God. This love and obedience to God instantly united them and sustained them during the trials they faced. It was the foundation of their friendship and were the ingredients that established their lasting covenant.1 Samuel 23:16 states, "And Saul's son Jonathan went to David at Horesh and helped him find strength in God."

Instant friendships are most definitely designed for instant purpose. Soon after they became friends, David's life was in constant danger. Jonathan was instrumental in saving his life on numerous occasions. By committing to preserving David and acquiescing his own kingship to him, Jonathan played a key role in preserving God's chosen nation of Israel and their future under David's reign. Even more importantly, by protecting David, Jonathan also protected the lineage of Jesus Christ and the plan of redemption for mankind (Matt. 1:1–17).

The story of Jonathan and David's relationship shows us that loyalty to God matters. It teaches us we must make sacrifices to follow God's orders, even when they conflict with what our friends or family may want for us. Jonathan and David's friendship also shows us that friendships ordained by God can be entered into without hesitation or compromise.

In worldly relationships, people are generally expected to prove themselves and show that they are worthy. These friendships typically begin under suspicion. That's so unfortunate because this type of ungodly mindset can deny us the opportunity to experience a divine connection from God.

There is one final thing I found very amazing about David and Jonathan's friendship; their age difference. Many scholars say that Saul was close to forty years old when he started his reign over Israel and he ruled for about forty years. Jonathan was already an adult and served as a military commander (1 Sam. 13:2). By law, Jonathan had to be at least twenty years old when he received the assignment of military commander (Num. 1:1–3). So, at death Saul had to be around eighty at least. Jonathan died with his father in battle, which is what ended Saul's reign (2 Sam. 1:4). This would mean Jonathan had to be at least fifty-eight years old when he died. 2 Samuel 5:4 records that David was thirty when he took the throne as King over Israel. That would equal a twenty-eight-year age difference between Jonathan and David.[13] Jonathan was old enough to be David's father, yet they became friends knitted at the soul.

2 things I got from this: first, we must learn not to judge leadership based upon the age of a leader. And, second, if God puts someone in your life who is younger or older, don't be quick to assume there is no possibility for a true friendship. Jonathan acquiesced to God's decision. He had faith in David's ability to lead because David had faith in God, even though he was much younger. Much like the relationship between Paul and Timothy. Paul instructed Timothy to lead the flock in the wisdom of God despite his age. "Let no man despise your youth; but be an example to the believers, in word, conversation, in love, in spirit, in faith, and in purity" (1 Timothy 4:12). Really the only questions that matter are:

1. Does this leader reverence God?

---

[13] Libronix Digital Library System; Logos Bible Software. The King James Version. The Bible Knowledge Commentary, Passage Guide:1 Samuel 13:1.

2. Do they govern their life according to His Word?

3. Are they steadfast and immovable in the faith?

Quick testimony: When I was a young teen, my oldest sister, Stephanie, wrote in my high school yearbook. She said, "Indeed Sissy, you are different. Your sensitivity and love for people, particularly older people and dogs is amazing! Your attraction to them is simply unusual!" It was true! I really did love people and dogs. I was always concerned about their welfare. I had a need to make certain they were alright. Because of that I had many elderly friends in the community. I was easily drawn to them as soon as I met them. I wanted to serve them and I also wanted affirmation from them, but that's a whole different story. After studying Jonathan and David's friendship, and despite some of my personal needs, I better understand now that it is possible those elderly friends were in my life according to God's will. Though the age differences were great, the relationships were no less meaningful and profitable to my growth and development.

The instantaneous nature of David and Jonathan's friendship was special and something many over the ages have revered. However, there is no greater example of instant bonding in love and friendship than that found when we are called by our Lord and Savior Jesus Christ. The term irresistible grace comes to mind. Irresistible grace means we are unable to refute His call and negate His teachings. Our hearts are made to be unable to resist Him. It is this grace that instantly connects us with Jesus in eternal purpose.

The doctrine of irresistible grace recognizes that the Bible calls man "dead in trespasses and sin," before being saved and the heart being regenerated (Eph. 2:1). The Bible further confirms we were once "under the dominion of sin" (Rom. 6:14). Sin's control and oppression are real in our lives. Man was spiritually dead and had to be regenerated and made alive in his spirit in order to receive the message of the Gospel (Rom. 6:11). Have you ever wondered why you might be trying to minister to a loved one or a stranger, and they look at you like a deer in headlights? It is because before you minister it is necessary to evangelize. John 3:3 states, "Unless you are born again, you cannot see the kingdom of God."

The doctrine of irresistible grace also acknowledges God's sovereignty. It shows us that nothing can stop God's plan in our lives (John 6:37–40). We were chosen to be His before the foundation of time, and we will one day give our hearts to the Lord (Eph. 1:4–7). The day Jesus determines as our day, He will draw us to Himself and we will not be able to resist Him (John 12:32). That is why we do not have to worry about unsaved loved ones. If they were elected to be with Jesus, they will be. Whether that happens in their final breath, or sooner, it is going to happen and there is nothing that can stop it. This is an assurance we have in the knowledge of the doctrine of irresistible grace.

Our hearts have to be regenerated so we can love the Lord and appropriately respond to Him. This type of response to those God purposefully places in our lives is what He desires among all believers. While our connections may not all instantly occur, Jesus prayed and asked the Father, "Father, make them one as we are one. Then the world will know You sent Me, and have loved them, and have loved Me" (John 17:21–23). This love is *agape* love. This love bound Jonathan and David in instant friendship and is the same love we are commanded to have for all believers.

We should not be suspicious of people God has united in the Body of Christ. This does not mean we should be ignorant of the enemy's vices, but it does mean we need to trust God's plans. We are to love freely as Jonathan loved David and as Jesus loves us. This is the distinction that separates us from the world. Jesus said, "By this love shall all men know that we are His disciples. By the love that we show one to another" (John 13:35). Unbelievers recognize Jesus' disciples by their love and acts toward each other.[14] This love is taught throughout the Gospels and is not optional. It is commanded to all believers.

1 John 4:19-20 states, "We love because He first loved us. If a man says, I love God, but hates his brother, he is a liar: for those that love not their brother of whom he can see, cannot possibly love God who he has not seen."

1 John 4:8 states, "Anyone who does not love does not know God, because God is love."

1 John 4:7 states, "Beloved, let us love one another, for love is from God, and whoever loves has been born of God and knows God."

1 John 4:18 states, "There is no fear in love, because perfect love casts out fear. For fear has to do with punishment, and whoever fears has not been perfected in love."

John 15:13 states, "Jesus said, 'Greater love has no man than this, than he lay down his life for his friends.'"

Mark 12:30–31 states, "Jesus said, 'And you are to love the Lord your God with all your heart, and with all your soul, and will all your mind, and with all your strength: this is the first commandment. And the second is this, you are to

---

[14] Libronix Digital Library System; Logos Bible Software. The King James Version. The Bible Knowledge Commentary, Passage Guide: John 13:35.

love your neighbor as yourself. There are no greater commandments than these.'"

Loving God's way positions us to experience great connections in friendship. When God unites us instantly to the soul of another, we should rejoice in knowing we're being set up for an opportunity to experience love at levels with friends we've never imagined. Let us not run from it because it is uncommon.

Chapter Four Discussion Questions

1. Discuss the type of love shared between Jonathan and David. Do you currently have any relationships that share that type of bond? If not, discuss possible reasons why.

2. What standards will you use to determine if your instant friendship are gifts from God?

3. Would you have remained faithful to Saul if he were your father? Would you have the courage to choose a friend over the desires of your father?

4. Does knowing the magnitude of Jonathan's assignment to David affect how you see your role in the lives of friends you know were sent from God?

5. What happens when you think your friends are diminishing your glory? Are your friendships able to withstand the reduction of your shine?

6. Jonathan laid down his ambition and rights to the kingship for his friend. Could you do the same?

7. Are you fearful of bonding with others instanta-
   neously? Discuss your fears. What is the source of
   your hesitation?

Chapter Five

The Transitional Nature of Some Friendships

"Henceforth, I call you not servant; for the servants knoweth not what his lord doeth: but I have called you friends; for all things that I have heard of my Father I have made known unto you" (John 15:15).

Have you ever met someone who you didn't like at first but, now you consider a highly regarded friend? If you answered yes, it is because some friendships are truly progressive. They may start out being casual acquaintances, but eventually grow to become Godly purposed friends. The scary part about these relationships though is that these slow-starting friendships are often aborted before they reach maturity. We don't give them the opportunity to progress because we are prematurely convinced they aren't meant to be. Unfortunately, many of us miss out on these God-ordained friendships because we don't believe there is any lasting benefit.

One thing is for sure, we do not want to be guilty of casting a purposeful friend aside because of our limited understanding of what God is doing. If God sent them, we must learn to allow the process of friendship development to unfold. This process makes these slow growing friendships very difficult because they require an investment of time and work—something we often do not believe should be a requirement of friendship. Many of us do not even believe they can be friendships if they do not come with ease.

Often, if they do not take on the form of an instant friendship, when there is no magic chemistry at the start, we mistakenly conclude the person is not meant to be our friend. But this is poor judgment and a total lack of discernment. That's why we need the Holy Ghost in our lives so He can show us spiritual things we will miss. Scripture says, "The natural man cannot receive the things of the Spirit of God, because they are foolishness to him; and he cannot know them because they are spiritually discerned" (1 Cor. 2:14). This means if we lack spiritual discernment, the ability to distinguish the godly from the ungodly, we will be clueless of friends sent from Him. Discernment is a gift from God and one we all desperately need when trying to determine if a person is sent from Him or not. Because friendships come in many forms and unfold in different ways, spiritual discernment is vital in distinguishing between those relationships that have God-given purpose or ill inspired intent.

In order to learn how not to cast friendships away prematurely, let's learn from the Master Teacher, Jesus Christ. What happened in Jesus' relationship with His disciples to cause it to progress? How did they transition from mere servants to beloved friends?

In Matthew 4:18–22 Jesus called four of His twelve disciples. The four include Peter, Andrew, James, and John. All four men were fishermen. Jesus issued a command for the men to follow Him. He did not allow time for the men to contemplate. He didn't offer expectations for their decisions. Jesus' command was issued as a directive. When we study the phrase "follow Me" in the Greek it literally means to "come now!" This suggested the four would travel somewhere beyond where they currently stood—both physically and spiritually. Jesus immediately gave the men a new occupation. He said, "I will make you fishers of men" (Matt 4:19). This phrase meant Jesus would teach them to evangelize and lead lost souls to the Gospel. That shows Jesus' investment of time and teaching. As well, to "follow Him" meant the disciples obedience would come with a cost. They would have to make tough decisions regarding their professions, livelihoods, families, and social positions within their communities.

Put yourself in the position of the disciple being called. Jesus has directed you to follow Him. You do not know Him well, but He still commands that you follow Him without giving any explanations. Wow! That would be a little scary, yet we see these disciples immediately leaving their nets and following Jesus (Matt 4:20-22). Without hesitation, the disciples abandoned everything and followed Him (John 1:43). You might ask, "how could they do that?" The answer points back to the doctrine of irresistible grace which made it impossible for them to resist the call. This is the same doctrine that will be at work in our lives if called to follow Him.

Once the disciples were on board, they immediately entered a relationship with Jesus with pre-established boundaries. The command for them to "follow Him" also meant He would now be their teacher. He would be their Rabbi. He directed the disciples to keep their eyes on Him. This command supports the one given in Exodus 20:3–5, which states "Thou shall not have any other gods before Me. Thou shall not bow down before them nor serve them. For I your God am a jealous God."

In that verse, "jealous" means God wants us to worship Him only because it is to our advantage. Our relationship with Christ, in the context of friendship, should be regarded as highly beneficial.

The command to follow God also lines up perfectly with Scripture when Jesus said, "My sheep hear My voice, and I know them, and they follow Me. No man is able to pluck them out of My hand" (John 10:27-29). We must remember that Jesus is God in the flesh. He orchestrated the salvation plan and predetermined what it would take to lead His chosen ones back to Him. That is why God made it that no one He called would be able to resist Him or reject His assignment for their lives. Jesus is the Great Shepherd and always works to protect His sheep. In John 10:27-29, Jesus is declaring His power to keep us in His care and established boundaries to keep out those who would seek to interrupt His plans. I like to paraphrase this passage of Scripture like this: "I am the Great Shepherd and you, My followers, are My sheep. You are to learn from Me. If you listen to Me, and go where I instruct, you are safe. No one can take you from Me." This is also the relationship Jesus shares with God. John 5:20 states, "The Son can do nothing of Himself, but what He sees the Father do: for whatever things He does, the Son does likewise." John 8:28 states, "I do nothing of Myself, but only as My Father has taught Me, I speak these things." John 7:16 states, "My doctrine is not mine, but His that sent Me."

Those passages show us that Jesus modeled the same behavior He expected of His disciples. The Father was His teacher. He received His assignment from the Father. He mirrored what the Father taught and taught the same to His disciples. His commands to His disciples to "follow Him" and be obedient to His teachings was out of protection and was intended to build discipline and humility. Their relationship with Jesus was not built on oppression or dictatorship. It was built on trust, loyalty, love, faith, and obedience—all of which He commanded at the onset of the call. These are the same factors He requires of His followers today. Once we learn to embrace them, we too will be positioned to transition from mere service in the Kingdom of God to an intimate friendship with Jesus.

In John 15:15 Jesus states His disciples were once servants but, were now being referenced as friends. Let's consider what was entailed in that relationship as we build the case for their transition from servitude to friendship. In this Scripture Jesus stated, "Henceforth I call you not servants; for the servant knoweth not what his lord doeth. But I have called you friends, for all things I have heard of My Father, I have made known unto you." This shows us a progression in the relationship. Clearly there was a time when He was not friends with the disciples for they were first His servants. The word "servant" is translated to *doulos* in Greek.

The word *doulos* means slave; a bondman; one who gives himself up to another's will; those whose service is used by Christ in the advancing of His cause among men.[15] *The Bible Knowledge Commentary* notes that a slave does not have a close relationship with his master. A slave typically has no idea of or involvement in understanding his master's business. The slave does what he is told and remains separate from the intimate affairs of His master. *The Cambridge*

---

[15] Libronix Digital Library System; Logos Bible Software. The King James Version. The Bible Knowledge Commentary, Passage Guide: John 15:15.

English Dictionary defines "slave" as a person who is legally owned by another and has to work for that person. *Merriam Webster* states that a slave is one who is completely subservient to a dominating influence. How do these meanings relate to the relationship between Jesus and His disciples?

The Bible teaches that we are the Lord's property (1 Cor 6:19-20), which is initiated at salvation by God's legal transaction known as justification. Justification by God simply means Jesus' crucifixion at Calvary paid and satisfied the debt for our sins and granted us eternal life with the Father (Rom 3:24-26). That is why believers can now live in right relationship with God. Justification is an act initiated by God that declares believers not guilty because the penalty for sin has already been paid by Jesus. Therefore, God's righteousness is placed on the believer (2 Cor 5:21) and he or she is declared justified. Romans 5:1, "Therefore, having been justified by faith, we have peace with God through our Lord Jesus Christ." This is God's gift of grace to believers, which is a result of Jesus' perfect sacrifice for mankind's' sins. This is why we now belong to God. We are His property. In 1 Corinthians 6:19–20, Paul says to believers, "Don't you know that your body is a temple of the Holy Ghost which is in you, which you received from God, and you are not your own? For you were bought and paid for with a price. Therefore, glorify God in your body, and in your spirit, which are God's." Looking at this text, we see that we are God's property and can be referred to as His servant. A closer study of Paul reveals that he often introduced himself as a bondservant of Jesus Christ (Romans 1:1). Paul was honoring the fact that Jesus died for his sins to claim him as his beloved. He recognized he had been rescued from a life sentence in hell because Jesus' blood paid the penalty for his sins. That's why Paul so passionately taught the Roman church that serving God with their lives was their reasonable service (Rom. 12:1). This too is the reason the twelve disciples were first considered servants. So, they started out as servants but, then Jesus' transitions them into the category of friends. But why?

Let's look again at John 15:15. It reads: "Henceforth, I call you not servants; for the servant knoweth not what his lord doeth. But I have called you friends; for all things that I have heard of My Father, I have made known unto you." The disciples had become His confidants. Implicit in the reason for this is the idea of transparency.

The word "transparency" is rooted in science. "Transparency" is defined as the allowance of light to pass through so that objects behind can be distinctly seen. It makes things or a person easy to perceive or detect. *The Cambridge English Dictionary* defines transparency as"something you can see through very clearly." Thus, if someone is transparent they are clear or easy to understand and recognize, open, and honest. Transparency is the opposite of deception, which is the intentional act of deceiving someone.

Jesus kept information from His disciples. He told them, "I still have much to tell you, but you cannot bear it now" (John 16:12). But this could not have been done out of deception because there is no guile in Jesus. So, what was the reason?

I want you to see Jesus' wisdom when He chose to withhold information from the disciples. This act did not come from a place deception, rather it came from a place of compassion and protection. Jesus had already revealed His impending crucifixion (John 12:32) and He shared one of them would betray Him (John 13:21). They were upset because they did not understand why Jesus had to die (John 13:37). And, they were deeply concerned about their own personal safety and well-being following His departure (John 16:17–22). Their hearts were overwhelmed. As a result of how they were feeling, Jesus discerned it wasn't good for Him to continue sharing. He knew they simply could not bear anymore.

Jesus' treatment of His disciples in this difficult time in their lives provides us an excellent example of how we should consider our friends. We must be compassionate and sensitive to their state of being in all circumstances. There are times when the information we want to share with them just has no immediate use. And, there are times when information is just not necessary for them to have at all. Having the wisdom to know what to share and when is vital to friendships. Unfortunately, we can be quick to talk and careless in sharing what could turn out to be damaging information. We should seek God's wisdom before we speak and always be sensitive to the emotional and spiritual state of our loved ones before sharing. Sometimes it's just a matter of timing.

I have known many Christians who become angry when they learn information has been kept from them by leadership. Unfortunately, this has led many to adopt a suspicious spirit and conclude there is no trust in the relationship. But most often they just do not realize withholding was for their own good. Sometimes, good leaders must withhold information because sharing it doesn't benefit the people they serve and love. Let us take time to consider Jesus' reasons for withholding information from His disciples before we jump to conclusions and needlessly damage the relationship. The love we are to share as disciples should express unity instead of rivalry, trust instead of suspicion, and loyalty instead of self-preservation.[16] Keeping these attributes will restrict us from reacting under the vices of Satan.

Another great example of God withholding for our own good is found in the Garden of Eden. God did not forbid Adam and Eve from eating fruit off the tree of knowledge because He was being deceptive or tricky. He was protecting Adam and Eve from experiencing evil they couldn't handle. That withheld information came from a place of love and compassion.

We must ask ourselves why we are so quick to reach negative conclusions when we feel left out of a conversation. I strongly believe it is because in some way many of us suffer from fear of rejection. So, every time we're not included in a conversation, we immediately decide we are being left out. Our minds tell us to be suspicious and on guard because there must be some reason for the perceived alienation. When that thought takes over, ask God to examine your heart so you don't live the rest of your life with skepticism and anger. If you do not resolve your feelings of rejection, transparency will never be part of your testimony because living in transparency is a sign of freedom from the bondage of sin. As long as you allow your mind to be engulfed by demonic thoughts, you will live under Satan's oppression and will not be free to love without restraint.

When Jesus transitioned His relationship with His disciples from servants to friends, there were some critical factors in place: His love for them was perfect and eternal. The disciples had spent years of intimacy and learning of Him together. And, Jesus had been transparent by sharing all He had received from the Father. That disclosure assured the

---

[16] Expositor's Bible Commentary; The New International Version. Frank Gaebelein, General Editor. John and Acts, p.153. Passage Guide: John 15:12-13.

disciples of their security in relationship with Him. As the *Expositor's Bible Commentary* says, Jesus assured the disciples of His love for them and showed them how they should love each other. As a result, it was Jesus' determination that it was time for their relationship with Him to shift from servitude to friendship. The time had come for Jesus to elevate His disciples from servants to partners, or friends in ministry. They had reached a place of maturity in love and partnership in service and were now prepared to continue as companions of mutual esteem and affection.

Chapter Five Discussion Questions

1. Have you experienced a true, Godly friendship that transitioned from one stage to another? Recount the initial meeting and how events in the relationship unfolded to lead you into intimate friendship.

2. If you have not transitioned into a level of friendship with someone you know has significant purpose, identify the factors you believe are causing the resistance to growth. Find Scriptures that speak to the resistance and take counsel in them.

3. What does loyalty in a friendship look like for you? Do you believe loyalty is necessary for a healthy friendship?

4. Are you crippled by doubt or suspicion in your friendships? If so, why?

5. Do you practice transparency with your friends and loved ones?

6. Have you ever rejected what you now believe was to be a progressive friendship? Will you do anything to attempt to restore the relationship?

Chapter Six

Exclusivity Is Not Godly Friendship

"Again, the devil took Him up into an exceedingly high mountain to show Him all the kingdoms of the world, and the glory of them; And saith unto Him, All these things will I give thee, if you will bow down and worship me. Then saith Jesus unto him, get thee hence Satan, for it is written, Thou shalt worship the Lord thy God, and Him only shall I serve" (Matt. 4: 8–10).

Why do you think some folks believe they have exclusive rights to people in friendships and relationships? Has Satan subtly superimposed his selfish, controlling, destructive tactics into their minds? It is highly possible because he is responsible for the notion of owning and manipulating people (Matt 4:9). Unfortunately for us, he actively pursues anyone he can deceive into thinking the same way. Scripture says that Satan, "prowls around like a roaring lion, seeking to devour whom he may" (1 Pet. 5:8). No one is safe from His attacks. His ultimate goal is to steal our worship of the Almighty God and turn it toward himself so we will not live out our God-given purpose in life. In doing so, he opens us to all his deceptive vices; eventually owning our minds by placing us under his dominion and control.

But, the truth is, Satan does not own us. Only God has the right to ownership of His people for He created us for His purposes and for His glory (Is 43:7). Because God claims all believers as His, He is committed to caring for, protecting, and guarding us from the enemy. Psalm 121:7–8 states, "The Lord shall preserve us from all evil: He shall preserve our souls. The Lord shall preserve our going out and coming in from this time forward." These assurances can be found throughout the Bible. But that doesn't stop Satan from seeking to distract us and claim exclusive rights to us as his own. He uses deceptive vices, such as material gain, wealth, power, etc. to separate us from God and to draw us to himself. If he is successful at his enticements, and, sadly, he often is, he can influence our belief systems. In doing so, he takes ownership of our minds and often we don't even know it. That's why believers are encouraged to have their minds renewed daily by the Word of God (Rom 12:2). We are to take all thoughts into captivity that seek to exalt themselves above the knowledge of God (2 Cor 10:5). That means we are to resist them from becoming our authority and guide. In this chapter, we will look at this notion of exclusivity in friendship and these subtle attempts at ownership of people as a result of falling prey to Satan's influence. We will study the catastrophic effects of submitting to his vices; a process he begins by separating people from God – His teachings and commands. For he knows, if he can influence our minds, he can ultimately destroy our friendships and relationships (John 10:10). Prayerfully, by the end of this chapter, we will be able to identify any personal impact Satan may have on our friendships so we can make the wrongs right.

Matthew 4:8–10 teaches us that Jesus was led by the Spirit of God into the wilderness to be tempted by the devil. God is sovereign and uses circumstances in our lives so we can see what is in our own hearts. God did this with Abraham when He commanded Abraham to take his son, Isaac, up to a mountain and offer him as a burnt offering (Gen. 22:2). God never wanted Isaac to be killed. Isaac was a miracle child who God provided. Isaac's lineage was key in God's overall plans for His chosen people. The purpose of this command was so that Abraham could ultimately see whether he worshipped God or his child. God's demand for exclusive worship has never changed. Matthew 10:37 states, "He that loves his father or mother more than Me, is not worthy of Me. He that loves son or daughter more than Me is not worthy of Me." God's insistence for our love and worship leads us into the right relationship with Him and protects us from idolatry. If we are consumed by our loved ones and others, they may easily be put before God and occupy a place in our hearts where they do not belong. Children, parents, and friends were never intended to be gods in our lives. If we worship them, it is idolatrous behavior. In Abraham's case, God knew the potential for Abraham worshipping his miracle child and needed for him to see if that was indeed the case.

Just as God led Abraham into a heart-wrenching test, God also led Jesus into the wilderness to be tested by Satan (Matt. 4:1). God will lead you and I into similar scenarios so we can see what our hearts are capable of. When God does this to us, we must not allow Satan to convince us God doesn't love us and is not with us. God is always there. He will never leave us or forsake us (Hebrews 13:5). He will always provide an escape. 1 Corinthians 10:13 states, "No temptation has seized you that is not common to man. And God is faithful; He will not allow you to be tempted beyond what you can bear. Know that when you are tempted, He will also provide a way of escape, so that you can stand up under it." Too often we give into the temptation because we don't look for the escape route. Jesus, however, didn't give in. How did the Lord resist Satan's attempt at exclusive control over His allegiance to God?

The Bible says Satan "showed Him all the kingdoms of the world and the glory of them" (Matt 4:8). And Satan said, "I'll give you all these things, if you bow down and worship me" (Matt 4:9). Satan had the power to give the kingdoms of the world to Jesus. Satan also knew that when Jesus fulfilled His purpose at the cross, he would lose his power (John 12:31–32). So, Satan's strategy was to interrupt Jesus' purpose ahead of time by offering Him material objects and superficial power. The *Bible Knowledge Commentary* paraphrases Satan's intent like this: "I can accomplish the will of God for You and You can have all the kingdoms of this world at the same time." If Jesus had taken Satan up on his offer, Jesus would have been the King of Kings without His sacrificial death at the cross. If Jesus had fallen for Satan's tricks, God's plan of salvation would have never happened. Jesus' purpose would have been compromised and we would never have the opportunity to be saved from our sins and live with God in eternity.

Satan doesn't want us united with God in eternity. So, He appeals to our areas of weakness and vulnerability. Such as greed for wealth, fame, and independence. We are clueless to the fact that when we run wholeheartedly after these things, placing their significance in our lives above all else, we open ourselves for Satan's attacks on our identity and purpose. Satan said to Jesus, "I'll give you all these things, if you bow down and worship me" (Matt 4:9). Thank God Jesus resisted his appeals. He countered every offer by referring to the written Word of God. (Matt 4:4-10).

Satan's intent to steal worship from God for himself did not begin with Jesus in the wilderness. It began with Adam and Eve in the Garden of Eden. The Bible says, "The subtle serpent approached Eve" (Gen 3:1). Satan's cunning and crafty spirit confronted Eve and she took the time to engage with him. In the process, he manipulated God's clear instructions to her and caused her to believe she was being deprived of her right to have the knowledge of God (Gen 3:2-5).

Satan is still doing the same thing to us. His strategies have not changed! When God gives us clear instructions, Satan attempts to make us believe those instructions are open for discussion. This is when we need to follow the instructions given in 2 Corinthians 10:5 and reject any thoughts that seek to override what God has already spoken. Because Eve failed to do this, she and all of mankind, fell prey to Satan's vices. Her life was now subjected to the father of lies – Satan (John 8:44). He successfully deceived Eve into believing God was withholding knowledge from her that she needed. Satan slandered God's reputation and His holy and righteous intent for mankind by coercing Eve into believing she was being robbed of something good.

Eve believed Satan's plan was good for her, so she disobeyed God's orders and sought to acquire knowledge that would make her a god. By disobeying God, Eve became the first person to try to take exclusive control over herself. Anytime we rebel against the Word of God, we are seeking to be our own god in our lives.

Look at the similarities in Satan's antics with Eve and Jesus. First, Satan appealed to their physical appetites. The tree was loaded with fruit, so it looked good to Eve (Gen 3:6). Jesus had fasted for forty days and nights and was hungry when Satan came (Matt. 4:2–4). The lesson here is to be careful how we respond when we are depleted, tired, and hungry. This is when we are most vulnerable. The flesh wants to be appeased and feels it is entitled to be so.

Second, Satan appealed to the human desire for personal gain. With Eve, Satan promised that she would have the knowledge of good and evil. She would even become as a god in her own life (Gen. 3:5–6). With Jesus, Satan promised Him the kingdoms of the world, but at the expense of His worship (Matt. 4:8-9).

What is our lesson? We must embrace Jesus' words found in Matthew 6:33, which states, "Seek ye first the kingdom of God, and His righteousness, and all these other things shall be added unto you." When we put God first and learn of His righteousness and truth, He promises to provide the things we have need of. Trusting God helps us avoid being easily enticed by thoughts of notoriety, fame, position, and perceived power. If something does not come from God, it is nothing more than Satan's plot to control our time and ability to commit to kingdom work. The farther he can draw us away from God, the more capable he is of conquering, and eventually owning our worship and allegiance to God.

Third, Satan appealed to the notion of an easy path to power and glory. Eve only had to disobey God one time and all the notoriety and control would be hers. All Satan asked of Jesus was to bow down and worship him. He makes the enticements look very easy and harmless; while all along his intent is to be destructive and divisive. There is a high price pay when you're under Satan's influence because he only seeks to kill, steal, and destroy our purpose and relationship with God (John 10:10). He is great at making bad look good, evil look righteous, and hate look like love. This is why he is known as the "father of lies" (John 8:44). He is a master of deception.

It has always been Satan's tactic to pull the veil of darkness over our eyes. He disguises himself so we do not know who he is. He works through family, friends, bosses, teachers, and even children. That's why Jesus warned His disciples, "Beware of false teachers who come disguised as harmless sheep but inside are ravenous wolves" (Matt. 7:15). If you know anything about wolves and sheep, you know it is the wolf's intent to destroy the sheep.

Satan wants exclusive control over those he seeks and has successfully imposed this way of thinking into the minds of many people. As a matter of fact, he has convinced them they are entitled to exclusive control of their own lives and often the lives of others. By convincing them they have a right to this entitlement, he leads them on a path of destruction (Pro 14:12). These people are in bondage because they are under the dominion of Satan. He is only seeking to separate them from God, their purpose and people. Have you ever had a friend with a controlling spirit? They seek to control you, their spouses, children, futures, and anything else in their lives. They make themselves the center of attention and demand others comply with their wishes. This manner of living is idolatrous and is in conflict with God's order. Idolatry is the worship of idols, which can come in various forms, including yourself, friends, spouses, children, jobs, fame, notoriety, and more. When Satan is successful at getting people to become their own gods, he sets them up to control their own lives and everything that pertains to it. This causes them to reject God's sovereignty and Lordship over them; which, ultimately, separates them from His presence, as was the case with Eve who was evicted from the Garden of Eden, the paradise for her life and place of communion with God (Gen 3:23).

If you are a control freak over yourself and others, demand exclusive attention in friendships and other relationships, and are passionate about your entitlement to do so, I am so glad you are reading this book. There is great hope because the remainder of this chapter will expose the catastrophic outcomes of that behavior and help you redirect your thinking back into alignment with God's intent for the relationships.

Ownership and exclusivity in friendship can be properly equated to a spirit of control. Ownership expresses exclusive rights over property, land, or something else. Ownership is self-serving because the owner holds the exclusive benefits and rights of that property. When something is exclusive, it is restricted, unshared, and off limits. If I own something, it is exclusively mine. I have control over it, use it the way I deem beneficial to me, have access to it when I want it, have sole rights to anything I wish to do with it, and I can keep it or give it away at will.

Now let's consider this as it pertains to friends. If we desire an exclusive friendship, we desire control over someone. We have the ability to manipulate them, use them to our advantage, and dispose of them at will. These exclusive friendships are sometimes deemed to be special because of the attention and perceived benefit received. Because of the seemingly special treatment, getting what you want when you want it because you're in control of it, this can easily escalate into no desire to share a particular person with others. This type of exclusivity can lead to idolatry within the friendship because the controlling party desires personal worship and praise and the victim is responsive to the request. This behavior mirrors Satan's blueprint for relationships: He seeks to own us exclusively by separating us from God; in this model between friends, those controlling the situation are seeking to separate their exclusive friend from others; and the one being manipulated is following along in worship and praise.

If we desire this behavior in friendships, we are more than likely suffering from an abandonment issue that was never resolved. When we fear people will leave us, we may have the tendency to hold on tight to them. As well, if we have experienced rejection and suffered unhealed pain from it, we will intensify the grip on those we think we can control. For then we will not have to endure the probability of rejection from anyone else. This oppressive treatment of people is not from God, it is from Satan (Acts 10:38). This Scripture teaches us that God anointed Jesus to heal all those who were oppressed by the devil. Jesus did not practice exclusivity. When He came to us as a precious gift from the Father, He did not come exclusively to one person (John 3:16). He is not an exclusive, best friend to one. He is a friend to all that obey His teachings and commands (John 15:14). There's more than enough of Jesus to go around.

Let's look at the concept of best friends more closely because it is common among many of us to refer to one or another as such. Young children often gravitate toward the notion of having a best friend or a personal companion they feel they can confide in and rely on to share daily life experiences. But, what we didn't concern ourselves with as children was that a best friend can lead to the concept of exclusivity in friendship. In my research for this book, I came across an article entitled, *More than BFFs: When Friendship Goes Too Far,* by Kelly Needham. Kelly described best friends as "people who act as functional saviors." They are there to rescue us from life's trials and tribulations, and they are people we feel we belong with and should be committed to forever. No one but Jesus is going to be in our lives forever. We only have one Savior. To place people in that position is idolatrous. That's why the entire notion of a best friend for life makes no sense. The article also stated, "followers of Christ find many benefits in friendship, but *identity* and *security* should not be named among them." [17]

Any time we look for identity and security from someone else, we should expect major problems. People who do not know their worth in God's eyes are not typically satisfied with their lives. I recently read a book entitled, *"I Hate My Life,"* actually written by my Bishop, the Rev. Dr. Jacqueline E. McCullough. She breaks down the issues that stem from discontentment and dissatisfaction. While people may serve God in outward gladness, deep in their souls, many are lonely and depressed feeling insecure and starving for identity. They grow to need certain people's affirmation and when they give it, they hold onto them as if they have exclusive rights to them. They can actually become territorial in matters pertaining to sharing them.

It is natural for individuals of the same sex to be friends with each other, so we see that closeness as normal and see no harm in the relationship. However, when the spirits of control, exclusivity, and territorialism creep in, we need to take a closer look. As Kelly Needham put it, "Since same-sex friendships are common and necessary for our spiritual growth, it is very easy to assume they pose no threat to our purpose and walk with the Lord. However, when they

---

[17] www.DesiringGod.org; More Than BFF's: *When Friendship Goes Too Far*; Kelly Neidham, March 1, 2017.

turn idolatrous and the worship of one another occurs, the friendship can become a danger to the health of a person's soul, no matter how harmless the idol may initially appear to be." [18] There are definite warning signs to be aware of: when possessiveness and exclusive friendship rights ensue, people will often find the need to defend their special friendship. They will feel compelled to define their friendship to others because deep inside they realize it is unusual and inordinate. Secondly, when people have a persistent need to justify the friendship in efforts to protect and preserve it, these are signs the friendship may indeed be unhealthy.

At one point I spoke with my friend Pastor Robyn about these kinds of friendships. She provided tremendous insight into the catastrophic, unplanned outcomes that may happen if the friendship is not realigned with God's intent for wholesome friendships. Robyn said to me:

> Many homosexual relationships are started because of same-sex friendships that seek exclusivity and ownership. When people live with deep insecurities and someone comes along who offers them continuous praise and adoration, they are responsive and may become possessive of the relationship. This worship doesn't mean they necessarily agree on everything, but what it looks like is this: I'll always be there for you. I'll never leave nor forsake you. I've got your back. I share my intimate secrets with you and you share yours back. We have a unique friendship that no one can separate. In some cases, you will

---

[18] Ibid

find these people will gravitate to these types of friendships and prefer them over spouses, children, and many others who genuinely love them and are concerned for their well-being. This is when you know trouble is afoot. This preference is the direct result of exclusivity. Then they will graduate into spending private time together excluding others. They will want to sleep together and rub each other in ways they think are encouraging and reassuring. Not knowing, Satan has set this up to lead to inordinate affection and, ultimately, destruction of reputation and purpose. Before they know it, they are in an ungodly relationship and do not know how they got there! It is because they brought their pain to each other and not God. Pain does not need to be rubbed, it needs to be healed! Anger and disappointment at the hands of rejection does not need to be embraced, it needs to be understood as a part of the Christian life. In many cases, if we are walking with the Lord, the rejection wasn't even directed towards us, it was directed towards God. We just happened to catch the brunt!

Robyn's words reminded me of what Jesus said to His disciples, "Whoever listens to you listens to Me; and whoever rejects you, rejects Me, and if they reject Me, they reject God who sent Me" (Luke 10:16).

Robyn continued:

The rejection may also have been the result of the ungodliness of the friendship in the first place. God ended it and these people choose to mourn over what He did to preserve them. They respond by acting confused, hurt and angry. These issues do not need to be cuddled by anyone, they need to be reckoned with through prayer and proper Biblical counseling. That's where true healing comes from. If they refuse the healing, they will remain the target for another exclusive, unhealthy, ungodly friendship!

Insecurities can be eliminated by a greater understanding of God's purpose and our identity in God. Since we are careless and do not know the wiles of the enemy, we fall right into Satan's traps (Eph 6:11).

Committed Bible believing Christians do not set out to become homosexual. However, when they do not see the Bible as the only source of strength, identity, and purpose, they become open prey. Not many Christians understand God's numerous lessons on the sacred nature of gender roles and sexual orientation. This ignorance of God's teachings may easily lead to carelessness and vulnerability. I came across a Scripture that blew my mind in this regard. And, I must admit, I had ignorantly practiced exactly what the Scripture warns against. Check out this example:

Sometimes, wives like to wear their husbands' t-shirts or jackets; even sweatpants around the house on a cold night. This may appear perfectly harmless and doesn't seem to pose any threat of any kind to our spiritual health and well-being. However, Deuteronomy 22:5 states, "The woman shall not wear that which pertaineth unto a man, neither shall a man put on a woman's garment: for all that do so are abomination unto the Lord thy God." The *Bible Knowledge Commentary* explains this Scripture like this: "The adoption of clothing of the opposite sex was forbidden because it obscured the distinction of gender and thus, violated the created order of life (Gen 1:27). It also was associated with the promotion of homosexuality." This Scripture in Deuteronomy reiterates God's intent to protect His people from inordinate, ungodly relationships.

You may be asking how an innocent gesture of wearing a spouse's t-shirt could lead to inordinate acts of affection with the same sex. But what we must recognize is Satan is subtle and God is careful. Satan is deceptive and God is clear. Satan has destruction in mind and God has the preservation of eternal life. It is the subtlety of Satan we must guard against (Eph 6:11). Further, all Scripture is given under the inspiration of God and is profitable for correction and instruction in righteousness (2 Tim 3:16-17). For Bible believing Christians, if God demands a behavior, we don't question the command. Rather we respond in obedience to His Word and reverence to His righteousness, holiness and omniscience.

Many of you reading this right now might be thinking that wearing clothing of the opposite sex is harmless. You might also say that same-sex friends need each other in intimate ways. If you are justifying your stance, you need to revisit the signs. You could be attempting to protect a friendship God does not want you to have. Boundaries must be established or the friendship will go in a direction neither one of you ever imagined. God instituted these orders to protect us. The bottom line is since the law given in Deuteronomy 22:5 was related to God's divine order of creation, and since God finds those who rebel against this order detestable, believers should willingly and thankfully take heed to the words of the Scripture. When we attempt to meet our needs outside God's divine order, we enter demonic territory and will fall prey to his destructive vices (James 4:7). It is inevitable and I'm speaking from experience.

In my early years I allowed a very distressed girl to enter my personal space. She was an only child and her parents— who she loved dearly—were going through a divorce. Based on this girl's extreme need for affirmation during that difficult time in her life, and my apparent need to be needed, our innocent friendship turned into an idolatrous one.

I became somewhat of a god in her life. I was seen as the one who could rescue her from her pain. She began to believe I would be there for her forever. A sense of ownership and exclusivity for my attention ensued. It was dangerous and deep in my heart I knew it. Our relationship fit everything I described previously. While I know I was called to provide guidance and counseling, I was not called to become her god. We must turn people to God and not ourselves. If only I had known then what I know now. When friendships become exclusive those friends become controlling and possessive because they think they have rights to you. That is why someone is left devastated, alone, bitter, and angry when the relationships end. They truly see the separation as betrayal. Without proper biblical counseling, the parties may never recover.

As God did with me, He will let you know when a friendship is heading in the wrong direction. I thank God until this day that He had His eyes on me, preserved my purpose, and provided a way of escape (1 Cor 10:13; Ps 124:7).

When God gave the gift of friendship, nowhere did we see anything about exclusivity with one another. It is important to examine your friendships to determine if they are exclusive, controlling and idolatrous. If you are questioning whether there is exclusivity in any of your friendships, and you truly walk with the Lord and want your life to glorify His holy name, consider Paul's counsel to Timothy: "Abstain from all appearance of evil" (1 Thess. 5:22). You do not wish to blow your witness to other dying souls! Just repent, reestablish boundaries, and place the friendship in God's hands. He's the best at reordering and redefining relationships.

Chapter Six Discussion Questions

1. Satan tricks people by offering material gifts and perceived power. Are you easily drawn by greed?

2. Do you believe you have a degree of ownership over your friends?

3. If you answered yes to question two, do you feel your life would be void of happiness and joy if you did not have these exclusive friends?

4. Do any of your friendships give the appearance that you are a couple?

5. Do you get upset or feel territorial when others are with you and your friend?

6. Do you find yourself justifying your friendships to other loved ones?

7. Wearing clothes of the opposite sex is considered an abomination in the eyes of God. What is your

response to this and will you make any adjustments in your life?

Chapter Seven

Friction is Necessary in Godly Friendship

"Iron sharpeneth iron; so a man sharpeneth the countenance of his friend" (Prov. 27:17).

The thought of having a friend in my life who would create friction was unheard of. I never could have imagined how that type of friendship could be beneficial or prosperous for me. This was one of those areas where I had a mental block. I struggled with the thought that a person who got on my nerves every day could be good for me, was assigned by God to be in my life, and would eventually become a treasured and cherished friend.

I was convinced my approach to friendship, my loyalty to my friends, and my ability to attract them was all I would ever need to know about friendship. I had to get to a place where I recognized that God saw my wisdom as foolishness. In 1 Corinthians 3:18–20, Paul admonished the Christian church to, "Let no man deceive himself. If any man among you seemeth to be wise in this world, let him become a fool, that he might be wise. For the wisdom of this world is foolishness with God. For it is written, He taketh the wise in their own craftiness. And, again, the Lord knoweth the thoughts of the wise, that they are vain." Our minds need to be transformed in every area of life before we can enjoy the fruits of walking with God. Romans 12:2 states, "Be not conformed to this world, but be ye transformed by the renewing of your mind, so that you will be able to recognize what is that good, and acceptable, and perfect will of God." The more we know about God and His expectations for our lives, the sweeter our journey becomes. When we come to know God's perfect will, our souls will be satisfied forever and we will not be gullible or easily seduced by Satan's wiles. I have lived this and know it to be true, especially in the area of friendships.

In this chapter we will unpack the idea that friction can be beneficial in healthy friendships. As we surrender our thoughts to the will of God in the matter of friendship, please keep this Scripture in your mind, "For My thoughts are not your thoughts, neither are your ways My ways, saith the Lord. For as the heavens are higher than the earth, so are My ways higher than your ways, and My thoughts than your thoughts" (Isa. 55:7–8). God's ways are far superior than ours. He is holy, and righteous, and perfect in all of His ways. His perfection is also true in the selection and nurturing of our friendships.

Let's begin this study by reviewing the meaning of friction. "Scientifically, friction is a force that resist the sliding or rolling of one solid object over another. Frictional forces, such as the traction needed to walk without slipping, may be beneficial but they also present a great measure of opposition to motion. The major cause of friction between metals appears to be the forces of attraction, known as adhesion, between the contact regions of the surfaces. Friction arises from shearing these welded junctions and from the action of the irregularities of the harder surfaces plowing across the softer surfaces." [19]Friction is the force that resists the rubbing between the two bodies that are in contact.

The imagery we begin to form is that first there will be rubbing, which is uncomfortable, may hurt, and will be annoying. Second, we begin to see there are two forces at work and one will prevail over the other. I'm beginning to see the mind of God coming into play. Proverbs 19:21 states, "The human mind may devise many plans, but it is the purposes of the Lord that will prevail." Do you see who will be on the winning side of this friction?

So, what does this mean for friendships? This portion of our study will come from Proverbs, which is commonly referred to as the wisdom book. Proverbs contains sound, godly advice and counsel on a wide range of issues. This book of the Bible speaks to issues of the human heart to provide God's wisdom and direction for our lives. Specifically, Proverbs has a lot to say about Godly friendships. Proverbs 13:20 states, "Walk with the wise and become wise, for a companion of fools suffers harm." Proverbs 18:24 states, "One who has unreliable friends soon comes to ruin, but there is a friend that sticks closer than a brother." Proverbs 22: 24–25 states, "Make no friendship with an angry man; and with a furious man thou shalt not go, lest thou learn his ways, and get a snare to thy soul." Proverbs 27:6 states, "Faithful are the wounds of a friend; but the kisses of an enemy are deceitful." Proverbs 27:9 states, "A sweet friendship refreshes the soul." Our Scriptural focus in Proverbs 27:17 is considered an admonition, which provides authoritative warning and counsel. The counsel is directed at both the young and old, so this proverb will provide wisdom to

---

[19] Encyclopedia Britannica, Friction Physics, Revised by Eric Gergensen, Senior Editor, November 2017.

anyone who reads the book of Proverbs. This specific admonition reads, "Iron sharpeneth iron; so, a man sharpens the countenance of his friend" (Pro 27:17).

What is iron and why would the metal be used to describe personal friendships? Let's try to answer by looking at the multiple uses for iron. Scientifically, iron is a crucial part of steel. It is a brittle, hard substance classified as a metal. It is the most abundant of all metals in the earth and is the fourth most common element in the earth's crust, comprising much of its core. [20] According to the Royal Society of Chemistry, ninety percent of all refined metal is iron. Most of it is used to make steel, a very hard and strong alloy of iron used expensively as a structural and fabricating material.[21] Iron also nourishes plants, and it helps carry oxygen to blood in our bodies. It helps to sustain life in all forms and is crucial to the survival of living organisms. Let's look further into the analogy of iron's use in sharpening friends. What does it mean to sharpen a friend?

Iron and steel embody strength and stamina. According to the *Blue Letter Bible*, the Hebrew word for iron is *barzel*, which means harshness and strength and denotes cutting. The *Gesenius Hebrew-Chaldee Lexicon*, iron denotes hardness and firmness.[22] If we think about those definitions in the context of friendship, we can probably agree that most friends are not typically hard and firm with each other. Cutting them with a sharp Word from the Lord is out of

---

20 www.livescience.com. Facts About Iron, by Agata Blaszczak-Boxe, Staff Writer, August 2017.

21 www.dictionary.com. "Iron." The Random House Unabridged Dictionary. Random House, Inc. 2020.

22 www.blueletterbible.org. "Iron." Strong's Concordance. Hebrew 1270. Proverbs 27:17.

the question for most. The Bible states, "The Word of God is quick, and powerful, and sharper than any two-edged sword, piercing even to the dividing asunder of soul and spirit, and of the joints and marrow, and is a discerner of the thoughts and intents of the heart" (Heb. 4:12). If we use the Bible as the standard baseline for our friendships, we will sharpen our friends on a regular basis. Since most of us don't do this, our friendships are fabricated relationships that have no potential to yield fruit. John 15:5 states, "I am the Vine, ye are the branches: He that abideth in Me, and I in him, the same bringeth forth much fruit: for without Me you can do nothing." If you grow indoor plants, then you can relate to this image. Branches are attached to the vine to receive nutrients necessary for survival and to bear fruit. It is necessary to cut branches on occasion so the plants can grow larger and healthier. According to the Bible, the same act applies to our friendships. If we are not pruned by the Word of God and teachings of Christ on a regular basis, we can stop growing and produce no fruit. Eventually, those unpruned branches turn colors, wilt, and die.

Jesus said, "It is the Spirit that quickens; the flesh profits nothing: the words I have spoken unto you are spirit and they are life" (John 6:63). Jesus meant that if we speak His words, we will bring life and light to the people who hear us. It is the Word of God that is used to prune our minds so we can continue to be strengthened and grow.

If God's Word is not used for pruning, there can be no spiritual sharpening and no fruit. Unfortunately, many people do not want to be guilty of cutting their friends with God's Word because they are not interested in being cut themselves! Many of us resist this painful process and would prefer to be left as we are. While Christians are to accept people as they are, the goal of Christianity is not to remain the same. We need to be sanctified so we can grow. That's what it means to be purged and sharpened; and we must use iron, the Word of God, to do it.

The Bible says we are to "provoke each other to good works" (Heb. 10:24). This means we are to stir each other up with God's Word, so we can be more like Him and righteous in our conduct. The only way to accomplish this is to correct each other when we think and act in carnal ways. This is often where we drop the ball. We think correction means rejection. So, we let behaviors slide. Satan convinced us that peace means no confrontation and no correction. He wants us to remain carnal. He is not an advocate of holiness or righteousness, and neither are we when we do not correct our friends in love using God's Word. The truth is, when we don't correct and confront, we do not sharpen.

In order to give you a true picture of a godly friend, I need to show you what it looks like when friends don't sharpen each other. When friends are not sharpened they become dull, flat, and useless. This should never be said of Christian friendships. If it is, it is because we are not submitting ourselves to Scripture. This is why, in addition to no correction or confrontation, there are several other reasons why sharpening does not happen in most friendships.

Sometimes, when friction arises in friendships, and our friends become difficult to love, we choose not to be bothered. But, when we do not love the unlovable, we are refusing to sharpen them. We would rather think those people are undeserving of our time and investment. That response, however, is not what Scripture teaches. The Message Bible translates Luke 6:32–35 to:

If you only love the lovable, do you expect a pat on the back? Run-of-the-mill sinners do that! If you only help those who help you, do you expect a medal? Garden-variety sinners do that. If you only give for what you hope to get out of it, do you think that's charity? The stingiest of pawnbrokers do that. I tell you, love your enemies. Help and give without expecting a return. I promise you'll never regret it. Live out this God-created identity the way our Father lives towards us, generously and graciously, even when we are at our worst.

Jesus commands us to live differently. We are to love and give as generously as Jesus has, and we are to extend that love to those we may think don't deserve it. Anything short of that reflects worldly thinking and an eye-for-an-eye mentality. The concept of an eye-for-an-eye came from several Old Testament Scriptures and references what was called the Laws of Retaliation. This is a principle that meant a person who had injured another person was to be penalized to a similar degree; and the person inflicting such punishment should be the injured party. However, this principle did not continue under the New Testament. In fact, Jesus says no to using this principle in relationships (Matt 5:38-42). Our love toward each other should not be retaliatory. We do not give to get and help out when things are convenient. It is when we love in the most difficult seasons in a friend's life that Christ's love in us comes alive. Friction should not be seen as cause to abandon the friendship; rather as an opportunity to strengthen it. Christians who never show *agape* love to others do a grave disservice to the Kingdom of God. As Jesus said in Luke 6:32-35, refusing to love like He loves us makes us no different than lost sinners. When we avoid opportunities to love the unlovable, no one benefits.

Unfortunately, the reason we abandon these friendships is because we do not believe friendship should be difficult. We don't think we should have friends that require our humility and mercy. What we fail to realize is that when a person receives love knowing they are undeserving, they are more inclined to do the same toward others (Luke 22:32). Opportunities to extend love in difficult seasons are aborted in friendship, no one is strengthened or made steadfast in their faith. No one is sharpened. The Bible teaches that the world will know us by the love we show one towards another (John 13:35). It is the extension of love in uncommon circumstances that differentiates us from the world. The love of Christian disciples is uncommon because it is not self-serving—it is for the benefit of someone else. The end result will always be the sharpening of another's countenance.

Another area we miss the opportunity to sharpen our friends is when we refuse to forgive them. A lack of forgiveness among Christians results in unfruitful friendships that do not represent Jesus. On the cross, Jesus said, "Father, forgive them for they know not what they do" (Luke 23:34). Jesus died to secure our forgiveness for sin. Yet, too often we ignore Jesus' awesome example of love and mercy. In the depths of Jesus' disgrace, suffering as a deceiver, He cried out to God to have mercy on the people who nailed Him to the cross. Jesus' prayer was not only for those who were physically guilty, but also for us. We are all guilty because we are born sinners. Romans 5:8 states, "But thanks be to God who proved His love for us, in that while we were yet sinners, Christ died for us so that we might be saved." God's forgiveness of believers was not based on us forgiving each other. Our forgiveness is sealed because it was based upon Jesus' sacrifice on the cross. A Christian's forgiveness towards each other is based on realizing they were forgiven themselves; when they did not deserve it! Ephesians 4:32 states, "And be kind one to another, tenderhearted, forgiving one another, even as God, for Christ's sake has forgiven you." A lack of forgiveness does not reflect the *agape* love of God, and it compromises our personal fellowship with Him. We jeopardize our prayers and our communion with God when we refuse to forgive friends who have hurt us (Ps.66:18).

People are made whole again through the power of forgiveness. They come to know that while they may have been guilty, God's love is far greater than their shortcomings. They will better comprehend God's love when they experience *agape* love through us. And, they will grow stronger in the Lord and be able to extend the same mercy toward others when they are hurt and disappointed in friendship.

The Bible assures us that offenses will come, but God has given us a way to reconcile. We should not hold grudges. It is unhealthy and can cause a number of negative medical conditions, such as headaches, ulcers, heart failure, and more. Our bodies were not created to carry anger. It is unbiblical and goes against God's command. Those who insist upon not following Biblical instructions regarding anger, are under Satan's rule and willfully ignore their responsibilities to each other in Christian friendship (John 8:34). Satan encourages irresponsible conduct and doesn't want anyone to benefit from the power of forgiveness. That is why we must be intentional and consistent in using the iron of God's Word as our guide in love and friendship.

This leads me to another example of a sharpening opportunity, which is a term called forbearance. Forbearance in secular terms refers to an agreement between a lender and a borrower to temporarily suspend payments. However, forbearance in the language of the New Testament means to bear with; it is a delay of punishment; it implies tolerance and longsuffering (Eph 4:2). Forbearance requires patience, endurance, longsuffering, and humility. It is necessary when friends refuse to change or be transformed. When we forebear with one another it means we stick with them even when the other person is difficult. We delay punishment! Forbearance is a major area of neglect in many of our lives because we don't believe patience and longsuffering is necessary in friendship. This rejection of Christian practice places a particular burden on the entire Body of Christ because if we do not extend forbearance towards one another, we abort the opportunity to sharpen each other's countenance, as Proverbs 27:17 instructs friends to do. Thus, we end up with a bunch of dull, fruitless Christians in the church at large which is counterproductive to spiritual growth. Believers, we have a responsibility to sharpen others once we have been sharpened. Jesus said to Peter, "Satan desires to sift you as wheat. But, I have prayed that your faith will not fail; and when you are strengthened, turn around and strengthen the brethren" (Luke 22:32). It is in friendships' difficult times, when we just want to give up, that the opportunity for sharpening another person presents itself. When friends are down and wandering away from their faith, Christian friends need to provide guidance and support found only in the Word of God. 2 Timothy 3:16–17 states, "All Scripture is given by the inspiration of God, and is profitable for doctrine, for reproof, for correction, and instruction in righteousness: so that the man of God may be made perfect, thoroughly furnished unto all good works." God's Word is our tool when we want to give up on others. It is the source of truth that will lead them along the paths of righteousness and break the bonds of foolishness. If they do not receive God's Words of instruction, correction, and reproof, because we are unwilling to forbear with them through their necessary seasons of growth, we are not fulfilling our Christian obligations in friendship. When we leave people in the mess they are in, then we are not committed to God's Word or the friendship. Proverbs 27:17 says "iron sharpens iron." This leads me to wonder, when we refuse to forbear with another, are we really made of iron? If our "iron" is diluted with anything, knowing it is to come directly from the Word of God, we are ill equipped to sharpen anyone. Our support cannot be mixed with magazines and worldly thinking if we're seeking godly change (1 John 2:15-17).

Lastly, there are times when we need to be disciplined, using God's Word, by a friend. Parents discipline their children when necessary just as God disciplines us (Pro 3:12). God disciplines out of love and for correction (Heb 12:4-11). As Christians we are also called to discipline our friends. This is not separate from the love, forgiveness and forbearance we extend them because the Word of God disciplines all by itself! Discipline sounds like a bad word to many people and may have a negative connotation because it is seen as punishment rather than correction. However, God's discipline comes from a place of love (Heb. 12:6–8). His wrath comes from a place of anger (Rom. 1:18). God disciplines us to create fruitful outcomes. Hebrews 12:11 states, "No discipline seems enjoyable at the time, but painful. Later on, however, it yields the peaceful fruit of righteousness to those who have been trained by it." Peaceable fruit of righteousness is the result of being corrected by God's Word. Righteousness is what positions us to be transformed back into His image (Rom 12:2).

When our thinking doesn't line up with Scripture and we are struggling in an area, it is fascinating when we share that struggle with a godly friend who isn't intimidated by the need to sharpen us. The struggle could be in the area of giving, forgiveness, forbearance, or any other command given to disciples of Jesus Christ. That friend may either offer a Scripture of correction themselves or they may say something like, "I believe God is going to give you a Word to clear your thinking on this matter." Or that friend may say, "You may not believe me now, but just wait! God is going to send His Word for your clarity."

Then, a day or so later, out of nowhere, straight from the throne, comes the instruction! It's often as if God was directly in the conversation! The Word is delivered and provides another opportunity for spiritual growth. This is priceless and epitomizes what is meant by iron sharpening iron; Christian friends sharpening each other. Disciplining our friends using God's Word is not abuse; it is love. We really don't love each other if we do not correct each other.

Christian friends are responsible to assist in the spiritual maturity and development of their friends. Just as parents correct their children so they will grow and mature, in the same way, we have a responsibility to correct our friends in love. Galatians 6:1–3 states, "Brethren, if a man be overtaken in a fault, ye which are spiritual, restore such an one in the spirit of meekness; considering thyself, lest thou also be tempted." Restoration should not be engaged in by people who do not honor God's Word by living it in full obedience. That is why restoration does not happen often. If we do not walk with the Spirit of God, we are ineligible to assist our friends. In Galatians 6:1, the Apostle Paul was instructing those who were spiritual to restore the brethren in the spirit of humility. Being spiritual means that we study

God's Word and govern our lives accordingly. Our level of spirituality is determined by our level of obedience to God's Word. Those of us who are spiritual are equipped to discipline and restore, which, ultimately empowers us to sharpen the countenance of a friend.

If we view correction as rejection, loving the unlovable as senseless, forgiveness as offensive, forbearance as impossible, and discipline as punishment, we will never position ourselves to sharpen our friends. We will be disqualified from experiencing God's design for strong, Christian friendships. For they require that we sharpen the countenance of our friends, using spiritual iron found only in God's Word!

Chapter Seven Discussion Questions

1. Do you end friendships that are deemed troublesome and problematic? Do you think only ease and comfortability denote friendship?

2. Friction is necessary in godly relationships because iron sharpens iron. How does this truth compare with your previous approach to friendships?

3. Discuss your understanding of what it means to provoke each other to do good works. Has this been the goal of your friendships in the past? If not, what has?

4. People wish to maintain their understanding of peace in friendship, which typically means no confrontation and no correction. Discuss your last experience with confrontation in a friendship. Were you able to offer correction according to the Bible?

5. Discuss how you respond to correction. Do you receive correction well? Keep in mind, the Bible says our Lord corrects the people He loves.

6. Offenses are common among Christians in friendship. Unfortunately, many times, they maintain the relationship without repentance or forgiveness. Why is forgiveness essential in strengthening friendships?

7. Forbearance is a discipline Christians are encouraged to exercise. Discuss what makes forbearance so difficult and why it is not viewed as a necessary component of friendship.

Chapter Eight

The High Price of Unreliable Friends

"One who has unreliable friends soon comes to ruin, but there is a friend that sticks closer than a brother." (Proverbs 18:24)

As we forge ahead in our study of God's patterns for friendships, I am fascinated by the varying degrees of friendships and our deep need for them. Now that we know God designed our lives with the intent of being in fellowship with Himself and others, I believe it is God's will that we pursue His wisdom on two additional matters— the number of friends we have in our lives and whether numerous friends work to our advantage or not.

In this chapter, we will examine a common reality among many of us, which is the desire for maintaining a lot of friendships. While we certainly do not all have this need, for many the absence of a lot of friends equates to feelings of isolation and rejection. I've known people who think something is wrong with them because they do not have many friends. And these thoughts begin at young ages in life. Just think of the young kid who sits alone day after day in the cafeteria because he/she is not popular and has few friends. The kid may believe they are socially awkward and don't fit or belong anywhere. Then they grow up and transfer these thoughts into adult behavior. They are apt to readily conclude they aren't capable of maintaining long-term or meaningful relationships and begin living as if they don't need friends at all. This type of self-isolation and withdrawal is not what God wants for anyone. It is Satan who wants us to live in isolation and depression. Let's see if we can determine why.

We'll study the term isolationist first. Isolation is the state of one who is alone, secluded, and withdrawn. It is the same as being separated or quarantined. Isolation is not a common lifestyle because it removes people from healthy interactions with others. Isolation is only necessary when there is a communal threat to life. When there is no communal threat, normal interaction should be maintained. The American Psychological Association states loneliness and isolation most often occur as a result of life transitions, such as death of a loved one, divorce, or a move to a new place.[23] Social isolation, as a result of these transitions, can have a profound impact on an individual's physical, mental, and cognitive health.[24] In addition, a 2019 study led by Kassandra Alcaraz, Ph.D., MPH, a public health researcher with the American Cancer Society, analyzed data from more than 580,000 adults and found that social isolation increases the risk of premature death. Interestingly, among black participants, social isolation doubled the risk of early death,

---

[23] American Psychological Association; *Social Isolation: It could Kill You*; by Amy Novotney. Vol 50. No. 5. May 2019.

[24] Philosophical Transactions of the Royal Society B, Volume370, No. 1699, 2015.

while it increased the risk among white participants by sixty to eight-four percent.[25]

Isolation is not from God and should be confronted. Anyone who voluntarily quarantines and secludes him or herself from social interaction should seek counsel. If you are a Christian, study God's Word regarding His commands that we congregate with people who are committed to living according to the standards of God's Word. We all need to be connected to a community of people committed to personal growth in God. Hebrews 10:23-24 states, "And let us consider one another to provoke unto love and good works, not forsaking our own assembling together, as the manner of some is, but exhorting one another and so much the more, as you see the day drawing nigh." The purpose for this fellowship is so we can be strengthened and encouraged. We all need it. If we are living in isolation, we are depriving ourselves of a basic human need.

My husband and I, our church community and the entire nation is currently quarantined because of COVID-19, the coronavirus. During this period, we are not in physical contact with anyone and only venture out when necessary. Even then, we practice social distancing from others. Nonetheless, though we are physically isolated, our church arranged to host our traditional weekly services and classes online so our church members can see each other, communicate, and continue to grow in faith. This interaction is necessary to sustain us in these unprecedented, perilous times. When the world grasps for anything it can to bring peace, we have hope and assurance through our Father's Word. John 16:33 states, "These things I have spoken unto you, so that in Me you may have peace. In the world ye shall have tribulation: but be of

---

[25] American Journal of Epidemiology; Vol 188, No. 1. 2019.

good cheer; I have overcome the world." Not only can we embrace God's peace, but we also have assurance of His sovereignty and everlasting care for us. Isaiah 54:10 states, "For the mountains shall depart and the hills be removed, but My lovingkindness shall not depart from thee, neither shall the covenant of My peace be removed,' saith the Lord that hath mercy on thee." In this season of great uncertainty, fear and panic, we must be deliberate about keeping the community together and encouraged. However, while our efforts to maintain connectivity among our Christian community have been extensive, there are those who insist upon isolating themselves.

Though some of us may be convinced living in isolation makes perfect sense, the lifestyle is contrary to God's will. 1 John 1:7 states, "For if we walk in the light, as He is in the light, we have fellowship with one another, and the blood of Jesus His Son cleanses us from all sins." Acts 2:42 states, "And they [Jesus' disciples] devoted themselves to the Apostles teaching and fellowship, to the breaking of bread and prayer." These Scriptures show that fellowship with each other is paramount to being strengthened in our faith. That is why Satan wants to convince us we do not need wholesome, Christian fellowship. His aim is to separate people from God, not lead them to Him. And he knows to target people who feel socially awkward and who suffer from abandonment, rejection, and affirmation issues. Satan is well aware he can make people believe that no one wants them and cares for them. In this, he leads them to believe if they remain isolated, they will never be placed in the position of potential abandonment. It would not be possible.

Whether we admit it or not, if we isolate ourselves, we become candidates for Satan's manipulation. He knows that without Christian fellowship, teaching, and worship, we will become spiritually malnourished (Deut 10:21). If Satan can get us to forget God by committing to a life of isolation, he can destroy our faith. Romans 10:17 teaches us, "Faith comes by hearing the Word of God." We must be in the position to hear the teaching and preaching of God's holy Word or it is impossible for our faith to be strengthened. Living in isolation negates that possibility and Satan knows it. His motive is always to divide and conquer. He is behind the spirit of division, while God represents the spirit of unity (Ps 133:1). Living in isolation as a choice to avoid the potential rejection of friendships is unhealthy to the soul.

Now let's examine the opposite extreme: Is it to our advantage to hoard friendships? To answer this question, we will study biblical truths about having a lot of friends. We will expose our motives for seeking many friends. And, finally, we will disclose the impact too many friends could potentially have on God's purpose for our lives.

We'll begin our study of Proverbs 18:24. This Scripture states, "A man that hath friends [Reya], must show himself friendly [Raa] and there is a friend [Ahab] that sticketh closer than a brother." This Scripture is often translated to, "One who has unreliable friends soon comes to ruin, but there is a friend that sticks closer than a brother" (New International Version). The New Living Translation states, "There are friends who destroy each other, but a real friend sticks closer than a brother." For our purposes, I'll quote the New American Standard Translation, which states, "A man of too many friends comes to ruin, but there is a friend who sticks closer than a brother." The common threads in these translations are the words "ruin" and "destruction."

Proverbs 18:24 is a challenging verse to explain because of the contrasting meaning of the word "friend" and "friendly." At first glance, we might take the word "friendly" to mean a person that makes him or herself pleasing; that a friendly person is one that is kind and pleasant to others. If this description is accurate, it would lead us to believe that in order to have friends, we must always please them, satisfy and gratify them. But, let's dig a little deeper.

Proverbs 18:24 is known as an antithetic parallelism, which means it contrasts the first line with the second to illustrate and reveal something very important. Take note of the 2 statements provided in the Scripture: "A man that hath friends, must show himself friendly, and there is a friend that sticketh closer than a brother." The word "friends" in the first clause in Hebrew is the word *reya*, which means neighbors, companions, fellow citizens, or associates. But note the drastic shift in meaning of the phrase "show himself friendly." In the Hebrew, this phrase describes a person who is an evil doer, or willing to be displeasing and injurious. By "showing himself friendly" the person is willing to be ethically evil, to punish, afflict, and break.[26]

The Nelson Study Bible defines "showing oneself friendly" as one who is willing "to beat up another; to bring to ruin" which most scholars agree is the proper understanding. So, we begin to see, by definition alone, that a man "showing himself friendly" means he presents himself as someone willing to be injurious, or even ethically evil. If we go back to the translations we cited earlier, we'll see a common reference to ruin and destruction:

The New Living Translation stated, "There are friends who destroy each other."

The New American Standard Bible stated, "A man of too many friends comes to ruin."

---

[26] www.blue letter study bible; Strong's Concordance. Hebrew 7489. Proverbs 18:24.

Let's pause a moment to talk about this because many of us desire lots of friends. We have this ideology that having a variety of people in our live assures us all our needs will be met. Many of us honestly believe that if one person can't meet us on one level, another person can. We sort of bank our friends. If one runs out, we can go to another for more of what we perceive we need; and, never be left alone. We are determined not to let our friendship bank account go too low! But, banking people to meet our needs is contrary to Scripture. Philippians 4:19 states, "My God shall supply all of my needs according to His riches in glory through Christ Jesus." Our sufficiency is in Christ, not people.

When a strong need for affirmation from many people prevails, it indicates a poor understanding of the character of God. When our affirmation does not come from Him, and we will not seek fulfillment of our needs through Him, and will inevitably turn to people. However, people are not positioned in our lives to rescue us from life's trials and tribulations. Only God can do that. To think that people are assigned to for these reasons is both idolatrous and unbiblical because it elevates their significance in our lives above that of God. That is why Proverbs 18:24 is really a polemic against a need for popularity; which is the state or condition of being liked, admired, and supported by many people.[27]

To be transparent, this section hit me hard because I have always been popular. Everywhere I've been, in all stages of life, I have attracted people. They seemed to gravitate to me. Looking at this in my professional life where I held positions of high leadership, I was certain many people gravitating to me meant I was effective, my interpersonal skills were sharp, and I had the ability to connect with people on

---

[27] www.google.com Definition of Popularity. 2020.

all levels. I was sure I was the standard of effective leadership, for after all, in my mind I had the ears of everyone I led.

Then, to prepare me for living a fully devoted, godly life, the Lord took me through a very painful reality check. At that time, I was serving as an Assistant Superintendent of Schools. I was in charge of all the schools and programs in the district. I supervised all the administrators, directors of programs, teachers, paraprofessional and support staff. This required me to work directly with lots of people on a regular basis. I was popular with employees at all levels, which was unheard of in my position. People thought I was different because I was compassionate to the needs of people, and I cared beyond what most of them had experienced. Then all hell broke loose.

The former Superintendent was arrested for sodomizing a child. From that point on, life was never the same. The arrest caused an emotional charge from every facet of the community. Because I was the second in command of the district, people held me accountable for the superintendent's behavior. They felt I was the one who should have restricted him from this and protected our student population from his perverted ways. Because they could get no relief from their anger, pain, confusion and utter disgust, they turned on me. Many in this once beloved community treated me like I had the plague. No one lent support. Few people called. None showed up to our public Board meetings in support. Suddenly, I found myself alone and scared in the middle of a scandal. I appeared in newspapers and on the front pages of our local chronicles as if I were a common criminal; a neglectful leader who had allowed something dreadful to happen. I felt like I had been condemned to be crucified at any cost. I was the sacrificial lamb! My mind went to the day of Jesus' crucifixion. The crowd hailed Him one day, and three days later the same crowd shouted "Crucify Him, crucify Him" (John 19:1–6).

In my case, the cheering went from "Pat for President" to shouts of "Crucify her, crucify her!" The very crowds that used to cheer for me were nowhere to be found when I needed their support the most. Just like the disciples left Jesus at the cross, all the ones I had mentored, taught, and supported, were nowhere to be found. I felt so alone and betrayed. I kept wondering, "How could they leave me in my greatest hour of need? How could they just abandon me like that?" "How could they drop me after all I had done for them and their community?" Unlike Jesus, my problem was that I mistook the people's appreciation of service as friendship. I misconstrued popularity as the loyalty of a friend. I misunderstood devoted service and sacrifice, to equate to entitlement and longevity. My expectations were off and it was no one's fault but my own. The people did nothing to me. God had to show me that popularity could not shield me from His ultimate purpose for my life. I had to be hurt and I had to be severed away from this false sense of security. That's why I can say from experience, popularity can bring great hardship because of its misinterpretation of stability and purpose.

How realistic is it that those of us who have been called out of careers, ambition and lifestyles, to serve in the kingdom of God, would have many friends? Does it make sense when you take a look at the many men and women God has used for great exploits in the Bible? Countless examples show how God separated people from friends and family in order for God to execute His will in their lives. In many cases, like the case of Mary (Luke 1:26), God separated people for a season, not in unhealthy isolation; but, for preparation for His assignment on their lives. Abraham was commanded to "leave his family and kindred" (Gen 21:1). Esther was taken out of her community to ultimately save a nation (Est. 2:1–8). The Bible teaches that those who belong to God will be set apart. Deuteronomy 14:2 states, "You have been set apart as holy to the Lord your God, and He has chosen you from all the nations of the earth to be His own special treasure."

Do you think a crowd of companions would have benefited Mary, Abraham, or Esther? Don't get me wrong, we need friends and companions. Ecclesiastes 4:9–10 states, "Two are better than one; because they have a good reward for their labor. For if they fall, the one will lift up his fellow: but woe to him that is alone when he falleth; for he hath not another to help him up." Proverbs 18:24, however, states, "Too many friends bring a man to ruin." Why is that? Because too many friends can distract us from our purpose. A large number of friends often demand time we do not have, create drama we do not need, and can be unreliable when the rubber meets the road. Proverbs 25:17 states, "Like a broken tooth or a lame foot, is reliance on the unfaithful in the time of trouble." This is exactly how I felt when I found myself in the middle of a scandal and no one was around to support me. I felt like I had a bad tooth ache! Nothing was capable of soothing that pain! But, though I was considered popular, those kind people were never positioned in my life to serve as my anchor in time of trouble. That's what made them unreliable; meeting my needs wasn't their assignment to begin with! The hell I experienced was not designed for me to rely on them. It was designed to turn my reliance to Jesus. If I had not turned to Him, truly my life would have been left in ruins.

We need to reexamine the value and purpose we may place on popularity. It is wrong for us to think that numerous people who appear to support us is the same as friendships on assignment from God. We need to ask some tough questions:

1. First, do you consider yourself popular? If so, do you believe the persons around you are in your life to support your God-given purpose?

2. Are you subjecting yourself to ruin and destruction because you think you need many friends?

Recall the first part of Proverbs 18:24 states, "a man that has many friends must show himself friendly." As we have previously discussed, this means the popular one is willing to be injurious and ethically evil. Why would this personal presentation attract so many people? Could it be the need for many friends is because of strong need for affirmation? Could the need for affirmation be so strong that we seek it from any who will give it? The truth is, when the desperate need for affirmation and acceptance rules our hearts and minds, we'll do anything for attention and support.

I already told you what it meant in my case. But, those people were unreliable in my time of trouble because they were not in my life to provide the spiritual support I truly needed. My mind was gravely disturbed. My spirit was vexed and my soul was captured in a snare. Only the Word of God was able to release me from this agony. My personal need for people to serve as friends and confidants in the midst of this tumultuous season in my life nearly brought me to ruin. But, that was no one's fault but my own. Popularity had clouded my understanding of who they were to be in my life. When those relationships ended, I was left with a hole in my soul. I had gone from popular to non-existent. My life hit rock bottom and I was left to start all over again; but this time, in God's kingdom. God had to sever me from all I once knew and relied upon, so He could fully align me with Him and His ultimate purpose for my life (Luke 15:11–32).

When purpose supersedes popularity, we will find ourselves with only a few true friends. That's why King Solomon advised us "There is indeed a friend that sticketh closer than a brother" (Pro 24:18b). Some scholars point to the use of the word "friend" in this clause as referring to Jesus, but that's not totally clear. What is clear, however, is that we need Jesus in our lives much more than we need people we mark as friends. It is interesting that the noun "friend" in this clause of the passage is singular. The definition of friend also shifts from companionship in the first part of the verse, to meaning godly love in Proverbs 18:24b. This word "friend" exhibits God's love toward man, His righteousness, and His chosen people. Because this friend is one who expresses his/her devotion to God first, their reliability and ability to endure hardships in life as a loyal companion and confidant are assured. This is the reliable friend who truly cares for your soul and will not abandon you in times of trouble. Proverbs 24:18 is teaching us it is better to have one friend who genuinely cares for the future of your soul than dozens of superficial acquaintances.

There's one additional truth about popularity I feel compelled to mention. When we deem ourselves popular, often we seek to reproduce ourselves in large numbers because we have access and influence over a captive audience. Case in point, in 1 Samuel 17 there is a great example of a king attempting to impose his ways on a protégé. In this chapter of Scripture, you will find a conversation between King Saul and a young warrior named David about David's preparation to fight a Philistine giant named Goliath. King Saul armed David with his personal armor and put his helmet of brass and coat on him (1 Sam 17:31-39). In other words, Saul said to David, "Go out like I would go out. Look like me and fight like me in battle because you do not know what you are doing." That made David uncomfortable. He was not used to fighting in that type of armor and did not trust it. David was his own man, and he was confident in God's power to protect him as He had done on numerous occasions before (1 Sam 17:37). David refused the armor, and instead armed himself with smooth stones and a slingshot, and was ultimately victorious in the fight (1 Sam 17:50). The essence of this story in regards to popularity is this: King Saul was in a position of great influence and had an entire nation following him. He had experience in battle and was popular because he was the nation's choice to be their king. Surely, he was accustomed to reproducing his ways in those men that followed him. This doesn't make him a bad king. But, it does suggest control over how his men prepared and executed in battle. David was different in that he followed the strategies of the Lord. David respected King Saul and revered him as king, but he followed God.

In my case, I had employees who were in subordinate positions, which gave me an opportunity to have tremendous influence in their lives. Thank God my motive was not to create people exactly like me. I respect that we are not supposed to recreate who God has already created. Our freedom of identity in God must be honored in all relationships. Godly friends do not seek to create "mini-me's." True Godly friends will point others to follow God, His Word, and commandments. That's what makes them reliable in troubling times—just like we have learned earlier from the example of Jonathan and David. Godly friends are clear, we are supposed to pattern our lives after God. They also know one day they will give an account for how they treated their God-given friend. So, Godly people handle their friends with care and cherish them for the gift that they are. The truth is, not many people like that come along in life. Here's a thought: Instead of looking to find friends that guard your soul and protect your purpose in life, focus on becoming one yourself. Then, you will not be a liability to people; and you will never be unreliable to the friends God has assigned to you.

Chapter Eight Discussion Questions

1. I've known many people who decide something is inherently wrong with themselves when they discover they do not have many friends. Have you ever experienced these feelings? How have you overcome them?

2. Living in isolation is not God's plan for our lives because it contradicts healthy, necessary fellowship. Are you, or do you know, someone who isolates? How will you help them, or yourself, going forward?

3. Are you among the many who have a need to be liked and heralded? Based upon the thoughts provided in this chapter, how will you address this need in your life?

4. How can many friendships become destructive? What have you learned based upon this study?

5. Have you ever wanted to superimpose your own character on other people? If they did not comply, how did you respond?

6. Do you have one or two friends you consider to be Godly and resourceful to you in time of need? If so, what makes them notably different from all others?

Chapter Nine

Reciprocity is Not Required in Godly Friendships

"And as ye would that men should do to you, do ye also to them likewise. For if ye love them which love you, what thank have ye? For sinners also love those that love them" (Luke 6:31–32).

This chapter will eradicate Satan's claim that we should give only for what we can get in return. Satan attempted to proposition Jesus by saying, "I will give you all these kingdoms if you will fall down and worship me" (Mat. 4:9). Many of us have adopted this same "give and take" mentality in our friendships. As a matter of fact, this mentality has greatly impacted the nature of most human relationships. People often commit to friendships and relationships with this expectation in mind, not even realizing its source is demonic.

The give and take way of thinking is so prevalent that it has entered the church and is perceived as normal. I know many people who actually choose their churches based on what they think the church can *do* for them. They look to receive but never to give. If they do give, it's because they want something in return. But that is not the design God has for our friendships and certainly not our churches. We all represent the church and are responsible for giving to others. Jesus taught His disciples to serve without expecting anything in return. Luke 6:33–35 states,

If you do good to those who do good to you, what credit is that to you? For sinners also do the same. And if you lend to those from whom you expect to receive, what credit is that to you? Even sinners lend to sinners expecting to receive back the same amount. But love your enemies, and do good, and lend, expecting nothing in return; and your reward will be great, and you will be sons of the Most High; for He Himself is kind to the ungrateful and the evil.

In this passage of Scripture, Jesus taught His disciples a fundamental principle of the Kingdom of God: What one sows he shall also reap (Luke 6:36–38). It's important to note that the return of the investment is promised from God, not people we call friends. We are not to give unto people for the purpose of what we can gain. We give freely because it is characteristic of the Father, and He requires it.

The give and take way of thinking is contrary to what we are taught in Scripture because it describes the act of reciprocity. Reciprocity involves the process of exchanging things with another for mutual benefit. "Emotional reciprocity exists when we provide empathetic support to someone, and when we're in need, that person meets us at an equal level to provide us with the same support. It's a mutually beneficial relationship with a balanced level of give and take." [28]

When we think with this idea of mutual benefit, we enter friendships looking for people to give exactly what we have to give to them—and, when we deem it necessary. If a friend comes up short, we have a problem, and often that's grounds to end the friendship. This response will negate the opportunity for meaningful friendships to develop because they end prematurely on the basis of unequal give and take. In the life of believers, there is a major paradigm shift that needs to take place in our thinking if we are going to govern our behavior on what is taught in Scriptures. The Bible teaches, ""And as ye would that men should do to you, do ye also to them likewise. For if ye love them which love you, what thank have ye? For sinners also love those that love them" (Luke 6:31–32). Many people refer to this passage of Scripture as "The Golden Rule" and paraphrase it like this: "do unto others as you would have them do unto you. If you love only those who love you back, how does that make you any different than a common sinner?" In simple terms, this passage means the life of the Christian should reflect the love and patience of Jesus Christ, and thus, be very different from the average sinner. God will place people in our lives for us to love no less, and even to befriend that will be incapable of giving anything back in return. Most of us recoil when God challenges our ability to love, be loyal and devoted to people that are unable to reciprocate the same in return. We often reject these people because loving others without the potential of reciprocity is not comfortable and we see no personal gain. Frankly, this book began because I

---

[28] www.google.com. Definition of Reciprocity / Emotional Reciprocity. 2020.

was forced to learn God's requirement to love and befriend some persons without expecting anything in return.

At the onset of writing this book, I found myself in counseling because I was feeling sad and disappointment with some people I considered friends. I felt they did not celebrate life's successes with me and acted nonchalant about moments that were important to me. Those moments were actually milestones that seemed to go unnoticed. I received nothing from them by way of celebrations or sincere displays of happiness. Since those friends did not rejoice with me, I stopped feeling the need to celebrate as well. I had allowed others to rain on my parade.

Maybe it would help if I shared a little about me. I grew up participating on cheering squads and athletic teams all of my life. I was born to celebrate victories. For years I worked as a high school teacher and coach. Working with people and encouraging them to reach their highest potential was what I did. I was relentless and committed. I am still a cheerleader and coach at heart. I enjoy team victories and see them as a reason for great celebration. I struggled with people who didn't celebrate others because I expected them to respond like I did. That is problematic for several reasons. First, my expectations were based solely on me as the standard. If I celebrate, you celebrate; which is equal to pride. Second, I had no regard for the reasoning behind their responses. It made no sense to me that great things could happen in the lives of others and go unnoticed and uncelebrated. I believed these people were my friends and that they should have been happy and celebrated. When they did not, I let their nonchalant attitudes compromise my joy.

My Bishop heard my disappointment and recognized my lack of joy. As a result, she called me on it. She encouraged me to go to counseling and to dig deep into my reasons for feeling so rejected as a result of my friend's lack of celebration with me. I needed to ask myself: Why do other peoples' actions affect me so deeply? Why is it necessary that they reciprocate how I feel? Then, one day, in discussion with my confidant, God put His finger on it. He said through her, "Trish, we are to do unto others as we would have them do unto us (Luke 6:31). People will enter your life that you are to befriend who are incapable of befriending you back. You are to love them, knowing they are incapable of loving you back." I was done at that point. I had never considered, in my wildest imagination, that friendship could be one-sided. I realized I had expected my friends to love me the same way I loved them. Since I was happy, I expected them to be happy. Since I rejoiced, I expected them to rejoice. I wanted reciprocity. I unknowingly embraced the give and take mentality. As a result of my friend's incapability to reciprocate, I strongly considered discarding them and felt fully entitled to do so.

I thank God for Biblical counseling because those friends truly belong in my life. I came to understand those particular friendships were not about reciprocity, but rather about the love of God being glorified in their lives and mine. I was not to receive anything I deemed as valuable in return from them. My value was to be gained from the experience of extending God's agape love, when I would not receive it back. Instead, I was the sole giver and have benefited greatly by trusting God's Word regarding this and following His counsel to love them and love them hard! One day I heard the Lord say, "I didn't tell you to bring them deeply into your space, I told you to include them in your life; there is a difference." He was telling me these were not the friends that would serve as confidants and "friends that would stick closer than a brother" (Pro 24:18). These were friends I was to include when I shared God's love, His bounty, His kindness, and genuine compassion. They were not to be excluded.

I had misinterpreted their purpose and nearly allowed my former beliefs about reciprocity in friendship to almost destroy what God had ordained. If that had happened, I would never have learned the invaluable lesson of loving in the absence of reciprocity. I became fascinated with this aspect of some friendships and began to better understand the mind of God around it. That is what prompted me to begin studying His many purposes for friendship throughout the Bible. I wanted to explore the tenets of friendship, the common denominators of friendship, and where I had erred in judgment regarding them. I was determined to get them right in my life, so I began this life changing study!

I fervently prayed and considered friendship in the absence of reciprocity. In response, God led me to study the relationship between Jesus and Judas. As we probably all know, Satan's influence over Judas led him to initiate Jesus' arrest before His crucifixion. But though Judas was under Satan's influence, he was on a divine assignment from God.

It's important to look at the name Satan as it was used when he entered Judas (Luke 22:3) In this Scripture it means "adversary," which describes Satan as the opposer, the one in opposition to Christ. Adversary is Satan's second name. The first reference is "devil," which means one who casts either himself or something else between two in order to separate them. Satan is the divider, the adversary, and the opposer who entered Judas. It was this same spirit of Satan that was upon Peter when he attempted to stop Jesus from going to Jerusalem. When Jesus addressed Peter's behavior, He spoke to the spirit of Satan (Matt. 16:23). Jesus was rebuking the spirit of Satan and informing Peter that in that moment he was being used as an adversary; an opposer of God's divine plan. This is the same spirit that entered Judas; for without this spirit he would never have been able to betray Jesus.

As the story goes, Jesus prepared for the Passover meal—the final meal He had with His disciples before He went to the cross. Judas was not excluded. Judas was one of Jesus' chosen disciples. But the irony of Judas' life was though he walked daily with Christ, he was not created to become a devoted disciple—only a common betrayer. That was his purpose and was determined by God before the world's foundation. Ephesians 4:18 states, "This one was created to live through the vanity of his own mind; one whose understanding was deliberately darkened; and one who was born to operate out of the blindness of his own heart."

Judas' assignment could only be fulfilled if he was under the influence of Satan. Satan's spirit of opposition had to be placed on Judas or he could not have opposed Christ. So, in my Bishop's words, betrayal showed up at the dinner table. After Jesus offered the true meaning of the Passover, He announced that His betrayer was in His presence. "Behold, the hand of him that will betray Me is with Mine at this table. The Son of man will go as it has been decreed. But woe to that man who betrays Him! Then they began to question among themselves who it might be that would do this" (Luke 22:21–23).

Judas was hand-picked by Jesus just as the others. The disciples were men Jesus called to be with Him. They shared intimate times together and grew to become a community. Though Judas' assignment was not to learn of Jesus but to betray Him, nowhere in Scripture do we find Judas ostracized or excluded from the others. As well, Judas' motives were not exposed by Jesus until the time had come for the final meal. It was during the Passover that Jesus announced to the twelve disciples, "the hand of him that will betray Me is at this table" (Luke 22:21). Judas never became a target of hostility from Jesus. Jesus extended love all the way unto the end. This is where we must ask ourselves a few tough questions.

1. Are we able to work with people we know have a vengeance against us?

2. How do we engage their presence every day in close proximity and treat them with compassion and kindness?

After the Passover meal, Jesus rose from the table and washed the disciple's feet, which also included Judas. The washing of the feet was traditionally a task reserved for the lowest servants. So, for Jesus, the Lord God Himself in the flesh (John 1:14), to kneel and wash the feet of His disciples was a sign of great humility and love. Though Jesus knew Judas was going to betray Him, He washed his feet. The washing of feet pointed to the total cleansing from sin that would be accomplished at Calvary. When Jesus told His disciples, they were not all clean, it was because He knew Judas would betray Him (John 13:10–11).

Jesus was charged to love a man who would never be cleansed. Jesus was the righteous judge while Judas was a dirty sinner. Ask yourself: Could you be gracious to someone you felt was lesser than you and incapable of doing the right thing? Would you be able to extend patience and forbearance to one you know has great dislike and ill motive towards you?

Forbearance is critical in learning to befriend those who cannot friend us back. This quality of Christ displays patience, self-control, restraint, and tolerance—characteristics of

Christ that many of us do not have or desire. But we are commanded to forbear with one another. Ephesians 4:2 states, "With all humility and gentleness, with patience, forbearing one another in love." Jesus possessed all these qualities, which is why Christians are to immolate them as well. Jesus had tremendous patience; that spirit that never gives up and endures until the end—even in cases of adversity. Patience empowers us to exercise the self-restraint necessary to not retaliate a wrong. Jesus lived that self-restraint. He had every opportunity to retaliate against Judas, but He never did.

Jesus knew Judas could not reciprocate the kind of love He had extended to him, but He did not withhold Himself because of it. Jesus still cared for him. That's why the Bible tells us that Judas' behavior deeply hurt Jesus. Scripture says it troubled His spirit as He told His disciples one final time that "One of you shall betray Me" (John 13:21). Jesus had a genuine love for Judas despite his disregard for righteousness. This deep anguish from the betrayal of a friend is captured in Psalm 55:12–14, which states, "For it is not an enemy who taunts me—then I could bear it; it is not an adversary who deals insolently with me—then I could hide from him. But it is you, a man, my equal, my companion, my familiar friend. We used to take sweet counsel together; in God's house we walked in the throng." They had walked together, eaten together, prayed together, and discussed kingdom principles together.

Judas did not realize the cost of his acts until too late. While he had received money for his acts of betrayal from the chief priests (Luke 22:4-5), his monetary gain could not pay for his sin. Judas attempted to renegotiate his wrong with the chief priests and elders, but they were not moved. He repented, but to the wrong crowd. "I have sinned in that

I have betrayed the innocent blood." And they said, "What is that to us" (Matt 27:3-5). These men did not care about the state of Judas' soul, the state of his mind, or the state of his life. They got what they wanted and were done with him. Their behavior towards Judas was the classic give and take mentality. They paid Judas and he gave them what they wanted. That was all that mattered to them. At their cold response, Judas threw down the money and went and hanged himself (Matt. 27:4–5).

The very person who loved Judas was the person Judas betrayed. Yet, the people he went into partnership with were the ones who betrayed him. Judas was under the impression he was popular with the chief priests and that they cared for him. He found out the hard way that those types of friends will bring you to ruin and destruction. Judas rejected the one person who would stick closer than a brother. We thank God for this example. Because Jesus stuck with that relationship throughout His earthly ministry, He showed us how to love a man who was incapable of loving Him back.

It should be clearer to us now that the only reason it is difficult to grasp the need to befriend and love someone who is incapable of reciprocity, is because we have been operating under the influence of the demonic principle of give and take. However, if we change the players, and take a look at Jesus' friendship towards us, we quickly realize we could never reciprocate what He has done. There is nothing we could ever offer Jesus that comes remotely close to His friendship and sacrifice for us at Calvary.

Going forth, it is my prayer we not be so quick to distance ourselves from people who cannot reciprocate what we believe we have to offer. Let us remain mindful that some of these people might just be executing their God-given purpose to lead us closer to the foot of the cross.

I pray you will keep this in mind the next time you are challenged to honor a friendship incapable of reciprocity.

Chapter Nine Discussion Questions

1. The "give and take" mentality is common in too many Christian friendships. Now that you have been made aware it is a demonic principle, how will you adjust your relationships?

2. Have you ever engaged in a friendship when the person you befriended could not, in your estimation, adequately befriend you back? Did you keep the friendship or end it?

3. Are you able to successfully work with people you are aware have a vengeance against you? If not, examine the source of your reaction.

4. Do you struggle with forbearance? Are you quick to terminate friendships once the person is deemed incapable of reciprocity?

5. How would you rate your level of patience on a scale of one to ten? What will you do to seek higher levels of patience?

6. Are you known for exercising self-restraint in friendships or are you guilty of retaliating against all wrongs you believe have been thrust at you?

7. Unfortunately, too many Christians have dropped the ball on modeling Godly friendships because they

are governed by worldly values. Going forward, how will you make necessary changes in your relationships to bring them in line with Scripture?

Chapter Ten

The Ultimate Friendships are Covenants!

> "Then Jonathan made a covenant with David, because he loved him as his own soul. And Jonathan stripped himself of the robe that was upon him, and gave it to David, and the rest of his garments, his sword, his bow, and his girdle" (1 Samuel 18:3–4).

Growing up, my twin sister and I had close friendships with two other girls in the neighborhood. They lived directly across the street from us and we went to school together. Our parents were friends, too. One of their mothers was actually at my parent's wedding and her husband drove my parents to their wedding that day. Both of our friend's fathers and our father served proudly in the military and that was how they initially met. Their mothers and our mom predominantly raised the kids and supervised the families' day to day activities. Both of our friends had brothers and sisters the ages of our siblings, so we all had playmates among the three homes. As children, we were extremely inquisitive. We were adventurous and enjoyed exploration and discovery. We were like little scientists and could always be found trying to understand something about God's creation. We loved the outdoors and, because we grew up in eastern North Carolina, the weather was conducive for us to be outside year-round.

Our inquisitive nature led us down paths through wooded areas and uncharted territories. We would not rest until we had opened new entrances through the undiscovered terrain because we were determined to find out what lay on the other side. We were architects and builders. We were intrigued with home construction sites in our neighborhood and always sought to determine how we could impact the project without being destructive or getting caught. When the sites were abandoned by the workers for the day, we went to work. At that time, we would begin our assessment of options to meet our inquisitive minds that many times involved dangerous exploits. I remember times when we would crawl into tunnels under newly developed streets and see just how far the tunnels took us. Sometimes we found ourselves under streets that cars drove on. Other times, we climbed onto the rooftops of homes under construction to find the best view.

We took so many risks, but we found fun and excitement in our ventures because we had insatiable appetites for exploration. Through all of this, we agreed on one thing: Our parents could never find out where we were or what we did. We were sworn to secrecy because we knew our punishments would be severe. In order to seal our oaths, we outlined consequences for anyone who broke them. We believed we established a covenant that would protect our secrets and preserve our union forever.

I presume our covenants were not binding because, while we dearly loved each other growing up and were committed to our friendships, they ended after childhood. With the exception of my twin sister, our paths never crossed again. So, did we really establish a covenant? What really constitutes the framework of a covenant? Do covenants have a lasting impact on our lives? Is there a difference between a covenant and establishing a secret society?

In order to better understand the premise of covenants, let's look at the first use of the word found in Genesis 6:17-18. Chapter 6 gives the account of God threatening to destroy mankind with a flood. Noah is introduced and described as a man who walked with God (Gen. 6:9). He found grace in God's eyes and his and his family's lives were spared. God assured Noah that He intended to destroy all flesh, but would establish a covenant with him (Gen. 6:17–18). The word "covenant," in this context, which is the Hebrew word *B'rith*, means a stipulation or a determination. The covenant was a treaty and an alliance of friendship. It was a form of a contract, which was accompanied by signs, sacrifices, and a solemn oath that sealed the agreement with promises for blessings for obedience and curses for disobedience. Covenants were possible between nations (Josh. 9:6), between individuals and friends (1 Sam. 18:3; 1 Sam. 23:18), and between husband and wife (Mal. 2:14). [29]

One of the most important covenants in the Bible is known as the Abrahamic Covenant. It was established between God and Abraham, in Genesis 15:18. The covenant refers to the land God promised the seed of Abraham, which are his chosen ones who remain under the covenant to this day. Genesis 15:17–18 states:

---

[29] The Key Word Greek/Hebrew Study Bible; "Covenants." Lexical Aids to the Old Testament, Hebrew 1285. Genesis 6:18. AMG Publishers 1991.

127

> And it came to pass, that, when the sun went down, and it was dark, behold a smoking furnace, and a burning lamp passed between those pieces. In the same day the Lord made a covenant with Abram, saying, "Unto thy seed have I given this land, from the river of Egypt unto the great river, the river Euphrates.

According to the *Bible Knowledge Commentary*, the smoking furnace and the burning lamp represented God who revealed Himself in connection with the image of an oven, or smoking fire pot, and a torch. Fire represented the consuming, cleansing zeal of God as well as His unapproachable holiness. The burning lamp represented the light of God's righteousness. [30] In the darkness, Abraham could not see anything in the vision except fiery elements that passed between the pieces of slaughtered animals. It was Jehovah, our covenant keeping God, who passed between the sacrificial animals and made the covenant for His chosen people with Himself. God knew that man, in his sinful state, would be unable to fulfill his obligations. Consequently, to ensure its binding nature and to make certain it would be honored throughout generations, God established it by Himself.

Covenants are understood as legal arrangements between two parties with the expectation they will be honored by those entering the agreement. The agreement is considered as binding and is not to be dishonored. Covenants cannot be aborted whenever participating parties feel like it. They remain legally binding regardless of the emotional or physical state of the parties involved. This is what differentiates

---

[30] Libronix Digital Library System; The Bible Knowledge Commentary. Logos Bible Software. The King James Version. Passage Guide: Genesis 15:17-18.

covenants from mere agreements. Their parameters bind participants throughout the duration, despite the inevitable inconsistencies of obedience and disobedience.

When I transitioned from my secular career into ministry, one of the major changes I had to make was no longer working based on a set contract, but rather based upon the content of God's covenant. What was the difference? Contract language establishes specifics, such as length of agreement, exact compensation expectations, insurances, specific clauses with respect to the what ifs of life, and more. Contracts also have termination clauses and expiration dates. Entering a covenant with God extends throughout eternity. The fulfilment of the stipulations are not contingent on my consistency or inconsistency, rather, the promises of God which are certain because of His righteous character. Deuteronomy 7:9 states, "Know therefore that the Lord your God, He is God, the faithful God who keeps His covenant and His loving kindness to a thousand generations, with those who love Him and keep His commandments." Scriptures like this, and so many more, have sustained me over the years. Numbers 23:19 states, "Our God is not a man so He does not and cannot lie. He is not human, so He does not change His mind." "Jesus Christ is the same yesterday, today, and forever" (Hebrews 13:8). These Scriptures provide us with the assurance of God's righteousness and consistency. This is what makes Him capable of fulfilling a covenant. All we must do is believe God's Word and rest in the assurance of our everlasting covenant with Him.

As we study the components of covenants in friendships, let's keep a few things in mind:

1. Covenants are established as legally binding agreements between two or more parties;

2. The execution of covenants is not contingent on feelings, rather the will to honor the covenant;

3. Covenants may be established as alliances among friends and those in mutual partnership; and,

4. Covenants establish stipulations and parameters, which are to be honored and respected throughout their duration.

It is a reality that many of us do not establish stipulations for behavior and boundaries in our friendships. Most often, once we become comfortable with our friends, we develop an attitude of anything goes and nothing is off limits. We often say whatever comes to mind and believe it should be acceptable because that person is our friend. We voice our opinions, even when they are not invited, about sensitive matters because we feel we have the right to do so. Sadly, this happens because we have no boundaries governing our behavior.

But, being a friend does not mean we have *carte blanche* to invade the space of another. It does not mean we have the right to disregard the privacy of another. On the contrary, being a Godly friend means we are careful to identify boundaries and honor them. The Christian's covenants in friendship and marriages are to be patterned after God's covenantal relationship with His chosen people. The Book of Deuteronomy is filled with exhortations for God's chosen people to keep His commands and honor His boundaries. Violating God's commands by doing what we think is right in our own eyes is a disrespect of His ordinances (Deut. 12:8). Just as we should not ignore boundaries established by God, we should not ignore the need to establish boundaries in our Godly friendships.

By definition, boundaries may be viewed as property lines. They are visible fences or walls that separate one thing from another. That means boundaries have a beginning and an end, which are distinctly noted. In the physical context, within boundaries, the owner of the property has full responsibility for what's in their jurisdiction. They are responsible for the management and upkeep of their property and there is an expectation that they will do so. The same is true in our friendships. We are responsible for managing our behaviors and keeping them in line with God's Word. In friendships, and all relationships, we are to remain in our jurisdiction and operate from a place of respect and honor toward our loved ones. Boundaries, however, are not established to keep a friend out, they are established to offer guidelines for them to come in. Without these guidelines, there is nothing in place to honor and the friendship becomes a free for all, where anything goes. That is why friendships fail and can end under really hostile conditions. It's the direct result of a lack of boundaries. Godly friendships should never function in this manner. Friends should be open to establishing boundaries because they provide benefits for everyone.

The presence of boundaries protects us from the uncertainty of our flesh. Setting boundaries has little to do with limiting others, its greater purpose is to establish temperance and control for ourselves. The word "temperance" means restraint and self-control. The presence of boundaries controls our own actions because they restrain us from taking advantage of others. In the absence of this unscrupulous behavior, friendships can properly grow. Many of us miss this benefit of boundaries, and choose to use them as walls of demarcation to keep people out. However, that's not the proper application of the word as it pertains to the Christian. Boundaries are established in relational covenants to protect the sanctity of the relationship, not to discourage them from ever happening.

Let's discuss another component of covenants in friendship; their proper execution. In our definition, we said the execution of covenants is not contingent on feelings, but the will to honor the covenant. This speaks of the need for *agape* love, which loves beyond feelings and circumstances. One of the many reasons so many friendships are unable to withstand the test of time is because they are governed by our feelings and emotions.

However, covenants cannot be properly executed when they are dependent on the uncertainties of flesh. That is why God alone established the Abrahamic Covenant. God knows man's frailties and that the arms of flesh will fail. This is why He sent us His Holy Spirit, which resides in the heart of every believer. He gives us power when we are weak. It is through the power of the Holy Ghost that we are able to honor God's commandments and successfully execute covenantal friendships. Because the Holy Spirit convicts us when we're wrong, when we cross covenantal boundaries, the power of the Holy Ghost snatches us back. Suddenly we are made aware we have crossed the line! This awareness and conviction of wrongdoing is what leads the believer to repentance and forgiveness. When that takes place, the terms of the friendship can be properly executed. If we allow the Holy Spirit to be the governor over our friendships, they will be able to sustain trials and difficult times. The friendships will not buckle under the pressures of life because they will be regulated by God's Holy Word and not Satan's demonic vices. Satan constantly wars in our lives, trying to get us to function according to his deceptive vices. Paul said, and I paraphrase, "I see different forces working within me waging war in my mind, my appetites and my desires. It is trying to subdue me and make me a prisoner of sin, which is in my flesh" (Rom. 7:23). Even though we all have this war going on, Paul states a fact we must consider in Romans 7:25: "If I keep my mind focused on God I will serve Him. But if I stay in my flesh, I will be governed by the law of sin." Today, as you engage with your special friends, ask yourself: Am I under God's influence in this or Satan's? The answer may revolutionize your friendship.

So far, we have considered the following components of covenants in friendship: the need for stipulations and boundaries, which establish parameters in friendship, and, the proper execution of the agreements. Those factors are most critical as we consider friendships that are Godly, covenant partnerships. We must also address the legal, binding nature of the agreement. This is the component that differentiates them from simple arrangements.

Since covenant friendships are determined by God, He is the sole enforcer of them. Have you ever wanted to run from a friendship you know God ordained? Have you tried rejecting its development because you did not want the responsibility of the friendship, but it seemed you could not get away? It's because God has determined, by His own counsel, that your friendship is going to be a covenant partnership. It is the will of God concerning the parties involved. It will be binding because it cannot be terminated, for termination would violate God's intent. Hence, termination will never be an option. These friendships are not simple arrangements established by participating parties out of convenience and preference. As a matter of fact, they have nothing to do with preference, but everything to do with purpose. God determined these relationships would be established before the foundation of the world to fulfill His purposes. He decreed them to be by His divine order, making them irreversible connections sealed in covenant partnership.

Honestly, I really never considered any of my friendships as covenants until I embarked upon this journey. It was only after studying a few biblical examples of covenant friendships that this has become real to me. I think by sharing some powerful examples of these uncommon friendships, all our minds will be transformed and those friendships that are ordained to be covenant partnerships will take on a different meaning and value.

First, let's look again at Jonathan and David, but this time we will scrutinize the friendship from a covenantal perspective. As a brief recap, David and Jonathan were united by purpose. Scripture tells us they were instantly knitted at their souls and their love exceeded normalcy. Because Jonathan recognized God's choice over himself for David to be king, he willingly acquiesced his kingship to David and entered into a covenant relationship from the initial point of introduction (1 Sam. 18:1–4).

King Saul, Jonathan's father, became insanely jealous of David because he felt his glory diminishing at the hands of his defeat of the Philistine giant, Goliath. So, he put David on his radar with the intent of killing him for stealing his glory (1 Sam 18:1–9). When Jonathan learned his father wanted to kill David for no reason, he grew angry and grieved for David. Jonathan supported God's choice regardless of his father's position and committed to protecting David. At this time in their friendship, Jonathan reinforced his covenant with David to make certain the terms of the covenant would be reciprocated in his family forever (1 Sam. 20:14–17).

Here we will begin to see that covenants are generational. Continuing the story, Jonathan and King Saul were killed in battle at the same time (1 Sam. 31). David mourned and lamented their deaths. He grieved deeply because he loved both Saul, despite the fact that he wanted to kill him; and he loved Jonathan. Shortly after their deaths, David was anointed King over Judah (2 Sam. 2:1–7).

After David reigned over all of Israel and executed judgment and justice unto the people, he remembered his covenant with Jonathan. He asked his men, "Is there anyone left in the household of Saul, that I may show him kindness for Jonathan's sake" (2 Sam. 9:1)? David was informed there was a son of Jonathan, named Mephibosheth, who lived in a place called *Lo-debar,* which in Hebrew means no pasture. It was known for being a place of no life. David sent for Jonathan's son and blessed him as if he were his own. He requested that Mephibosheth remain on the land of his grandfather Saul, and eat at the king's table for the rest of his life. 2 Samuel 9:7 states, "I will surely show you kindness for the sake of your father Jonathan. I will restore to you all the land that belonged to your grandfather Saul and you will always eat at my table." As we see, David's loyalty to Jonathan extended far past his natural life and covered the relatives that were left behind. This generational covenant patterns the design of God's covenant with Abraham and his seed. Genesis 15:18 states, "In the same day the Lord made a covenant with Abram, saying, unto thy seed have I given this land, from the river of Egypt unto the great river, the river Euphrates."

Our next life covenant example is found in the relationship with Ruth and Naomi. Join me as we review this beautiful blend of cultures, family backgrounds, and ages (Ruth 1). Naomi was a Jewish woman, well cared for with a husband and two sons. Her husband's name was Elimelech. The story begins with a famine in the land where they lived, Bethlehem. In the family's quest to seek provision, they decided to leave Bethlehem, the place of blessing, and travel to a foreign land called Moab. Shortly into their new life, Naomi's husband died and her two sons married Moabite women named Orpah and Ruth. They remained in Moab for ten years. Then, suddenly both sons also died (Ruth 1:1–5). Naomi had two daughters-in-law, but no husband or sons.

They were three widowed women left to fend for themselves. In this ancient culture, women relied on husbands for economic security and they desired sons in order for the name to be carried on throughout generations. Having lost all the men in her family, Naomi decided to return to her native land, Bethlehem. She insisted her widowed daughters-in-law both return to their mother's house in Moab where they could possibly remarry and be properly cared for (Ruth 1:8–9). Naomi had no more sons to offer them and she was grieving over how the Lord had dealt with her. So, she did not want the young women to follow her. Naomi urged the women three times to go back. Orpah decided that would be wise, kissed her and left. However, Ruth refused to go. She basically told Naomi to stop trying to force her in that direction. Ruth 1:16–17 states, "Entreat me never to leave you! Where you go I will go; where you lodge, I will lodge. Your people will be my people, and your God will be my God. Where you're buried, I shall be buried! May the Lord deal with me ever so severely if anything but death separates us." Ruth understood her relationship to Naomi was not about what Naomi had or didn't have to offer her. Instead, their relationship was a divine, covenant connection that had been established by God. Ruth knew this connection could not be interrupted even by the deaths of their husbands. Thus, she was determined to preserve and honor it. In her obedience to the covenant, she had confidence it would be God who would take care of them going forth.

And Ruth was right! God did take care of her and Naomi. Ruth went to work in the fields and was spotted by a man named Boaz, who was a kinsman of Naomi's, related to her deceased husband. Boaz inquired about Ruth and already knew of her commitment to Naomi and how she had cared for her in the most difficult season of her life. He stated in Ruth 2:11–12, "I've been told all about what you did for your mother-in-law since the death of your husband—how you left your father and mother, and your homeland and to come to live with people you didn't know. May the Lord repay you for what you have done. May you be richly rewarded by the Lord, the God of Israel, under whose wings you have come to take refuge." Eventually Boaz married Ruth. It was in this union the full purpose of the covenant between Ruth and Naomi unfolded. The couple conceived and had a son named Obed. Obed was the father of Jesse; who was the father of King David. In this family, Ruth became part of Jesus' lineage (Matt 1:1-17). Ruth's choice to stay with Naomi proved to have generational and eternal blessings for us all.

Finally, I will conclude this chapter on friendships as eternal covenants with my own story. For, I too have been planted in a covenant relationship with my Pastor / Bishop, the esteemed Rev. Dr. Jacqueline E. McCullough. Bishop McCullough is the under-shepherd of my soul. She is my Moses, and I have been assigned to a covenant partnership with her for life. How do I know this? God has given me this clarity through His Word at varying junctures of this relationship. To start, I came to know Bishop McCullough because of a recommendation from another reputable

Pastor who knew her well. At the time, I needed a church home. I had always had a church family in my life but, in that season, I found myself wandering from one church to another, seeking a place to land. The Pastor recommended that I find Bishop McCullough because, after sharing the length of time I had been wandering, she knew I needed teaching. Bishop is known worldwide for her integrity to God's Word and her teaching of the full gospel. I had no idea who she was and knew absolutely nothing about her, but, soon thereafter I would. The same night after the Pastor recommended her, I had a dream. In the dream I appeared in a beautiful, all white praise outfit. I leapt and danced down the middle aisle of a church. While I didn't know what it meant in its entirety, I did know because of the white, the location, and the joy in my soul, that it was divine, it was good and it was God. With that, I sought out the church, the International Gathering at Beth Rapha. The first Sunday I met Bishop McCullough, I remember saying, "I don't know why I am here, but I was sent." That was eighteen years ago, and I'm still there.

Like any relationship, over the years, it had to grow. Trust had to develop. Obedience had to ensue. Sacrifice had to become natural. I had to mature and better understand what God was doing in my life. It wasn't easy for me in the early years. My life and professional career of twenty-five years were stripped away in order to position me to serve under Bishop McCullough's tutelage in God's kingdom. I had to acquiesce all I had ever dreamed of and desired to do to serve this woman of God and her vision. That was beyond tough, but I knew deep in my agitated soul, I had to say yes! I was angry with God, disappointed, and confused. While I always enjoyed the church, I could not understand the need to give up my career to serve. Of course, I had no idea how the demands on my life were about to change. It was more than a church or a ministry, it was a community of believers God brought from various walks of life to collaboratively execute a divine mission. There would be a fully accredited Bible College and Theological Seminary, of which I would organize and fully execute alongside Bishop McCullough. Our ministry would serve as a headquartered church for over 20 other churches that would be led to align themselves with us in purpose and commitment. I didn't know Beth Rapha was a place where I would learn to rightly divide and teach God's Word both in-house and to people all over the world through the various technology mediums. And, most importantly to me, I didn't know I was exchanging my office of Superintendent of Schools, to become a true disciple of Jesus Christ committed to making disciples all over the world, for the rest of my life! I had no idea of how deeply the Lord would invest me in the culture and fabric of the vision of this ministry. And, I certainly did not know His intentions to bind me to my Bishop in covenantal partnership, with chords that could never be broken.

A few years ago, we celebrated Bishop McCullough's thirteenth year as Founder of our church. I asked God for words to share during the celebration and the Lord led me to the book of Ruth. Ruth 1:16–17 states, "Entreat me never to leave you, or to return from following thee: for where you go, I will go; and where you lodge I will lodge. Your people shall be my people, and your God shall be my God. Where you die, I will die and there shall I be buried. May the Lord punish me, and ever so severely, if anything but death separates you and me." After receiving this Word, I was so clear of God's instructions to me that it scared me. While I am unaware of many things pertaining to this commitment, I do know I am in it for life, and the Lord wanted me to be sure I got His memo. He ordained the unity to be binded in covenant partnership, and, it would be an alliance that would extend throughout eternity.

This clarity dropped me right into the place of agreement. And, to top it off, one of our brothers in ministry preached during a Founder's Celebration weekend at a time I was truly struggling with honoring this assignment. He said to me, "you're in the right place, and she is the right one!" I was done and have been ever since! I no longer wrestle in my spirit. I have settled in a place of obedience and contentment, knowing it is the will of God concerning me. I have fully embraced my assignment to the vision and truthfully thank God for it every day. Along the journey, I have met many Godly friends, and have been showered with numerous brothers and sisters in the faith, nieces, nephews, and godchildren. And, I honestly reap the benefits of saying yes to God's will every day of my life.

It is a divine order from God. And, as Ruth put it, "May the Lord punish me, and ever so severely, if anything but death separates us" (Ruth 1:17). Like Ruth, I was never after anything Bishop McCullough could or could not do for me. I wasn't seeking to be attached to her name or anything she had. But, I was after her God. Her people have now become my people, and her God is now my God. How blessed I am to co-labor with this awesome giant in the faith, forever bonded together in covenant with our God.

Deuteronomy 7:6–9 states:

> For thou art a holy people unto the Lord thy God: the Lord thy God has chosen you to be a special people unto Himself, above all people that are upon the face of the earth. The LORD did not set His love upon you, nor choose you,

because you were more in number than any
people, for you were the fewest of all. But
because the LORD loved you, and because He
would keep the oath which he had sworn unto
your fathers (referring to Abraham, Isaac, and
Jacob) hath the LORD brought you out with
a mighty hand, and redeemed you out of the
house of bondmen, from the hand of Pharaoh,
king of Egypt. Know therefore, that the LORD
thy God, He is God, the faithful God, which
keepeth covenant and mercy with them that
love Him and keep His commandments to a
thousand generations.

Chapter Ten Discussion Questions

1. Discuss what constitutes the framework of a covenant friendship. How does this differ from your previous understanding of "lifelong" friendships?

2. All friendships are not eternal covenants because
   many are seasonal, many will not have reciprocity,
   etc. Do you currently have any friendships you consider covenants? If so, how are you arriving at this
   conclusion?

3. In the case of Jonathan and David, a major part of
   their relationship and, perhaps one of the things that
   makes it very unique, is that Jonathan acquiesced his
   future for David. He literally laid down his life for
   his friend. Have you ever done that for another? Has
   anyone done it for you?

4. Jonathan's loyalty to his father did not blind his commitment to divine purpose. Consider how you may have handled this potentially divisive situation.

5. David was committed to caring for any of Saul's family members that were still alive, even though Saul tried to kill him on several occasions. This is indeed a case where he was honoring the covenant in their friendship. What would your response have been?

6. Naomi attempted to force Ruth to take another path in life numerous times. Have you ever remained in a friendship knowing the other person wanted you to leave? What was your motivation for staying?

7. How will your friendships be reconsidered after reading this chapter?

Footnote Page

1 www.dictionary.cambridge.org. "Gifts." The Cambridge English Dictionary.

2 *Coaching 4 Success; The Value of Friendship*; By Robert Lewis Stevenson. Prague Leader's Magazine; May 2009.

3 The Key Word Greek / Hebrew Study Bible. "Good." Lexical Aids to the New Testament, Greek 18. James 1:17. AMG Publishers 1991.

4 Libronix Digital Library System; Logos Bible Software. The King James Version. The Bible Knowledge Commentary, Passage Guide: John 10:10.

5 www.blueletterbible.org. "Elohim." Strong's Concordance, Hebrews 430. Genesis 1:27.

6 www.blueletterbible.org. "Good." Strong's Concordance, Hebrews 2896. Genesis 2:18.

7 www.lexico.com. "Help Meet." Oxford Dictionary. 2020.

8 The Barna Group; *U.S. Adults Have Few Friends.* Articles in Culture and Media; October 23, 2018.

9 Biblestudytools.com/dictionaries/bakers-evangelical-dictionary/friend-friendship.html; Friend / Friendship. Carl B. Bridges, Jr. Copyright 1996.

10 Nelson's Illustrated Dictionary of the Bible; "Terah." Herbert Lockyer, Sr. Editor, Thomas Nelson Publishers, Copyright 1986. p.459.

11 Nelson's Illustrated Dictionary of the Bible; "Sin-moon-god." Herbert Lockyer, Sr. Editor, Thomas Nelson Publishers, Copyright 1986. p.459.

12 Libronix Digital Library System; Logos Bible Software. The King James Version. The Bible Knowledge Commentary, Passage Guide:1 Samuel 18.

13 Libronix Digital Library System; Logos Bible Software. The King James Version. The Bible Knowledge Commentary, Passage Guide:1 Samuel 13:1.

14 Libronix Digital Library System; Logos Bible Software. The King James Version. The Bible Knowledge Commentary, Passage Guide: John 13:35.

15 Libronix Digital Library System; Logos Bible Software. The King James Version. The Bible Knowledge Commentary, Passage Guide: John 15:15.

16 Expositor's Bible Commentary; The New International Version. Frank Gaebelein, General Editor. John and Acts, p.153. Passage Guide: John 15:12-13.

17 www.DesiringGod.org; More Than BFF's: *When Friendship Goes Too Far*; Kelly Neidham, March 1, 2017.

18 Ibid

[19] Encyclopedia Britannica, Friction Physics, Revised by Eric Gergensen, Senior Editor, November 2017.

[20] www.livescience.com. Facts About Iron, by Agata Blaszczak-Boxe, Staff Writer, August 2017.

[21] www.dictionary.com. "Iron." The Random House Unabridged Dictionary. Random House, Inc. 2020.

[22] www.blueletterbible.org. "Iron." Strong's Concordance. Hebrew 1270. Proverbs 27:17.

[23] American Psychological Association; *Social Isolation: It could Kill You*; by Amy Novotney. Vol 50. No. 5. May 2019.

[24] Philosophical Transactions of the Royal Society B, Volume370, No. 1699, 2015.

[25] American Journal of Epidemiology; Vol 188, No. 1. 2019.

[26] www.blue letter study bible; Strong's Concordance. Hebrew 7489. Proverbs 18:24.

[27] www.google.com Definition of Popularity. 2020.

[28] www.google.com. Definition of Reciprocity / Emotional Reciprocity. 2020.

[29] The Key Word Greek/Hebrew Study Bible; "Covenants." Lexical Aids to the Old Testament, Hebrew 1285. Genesis 6:18. AMG Publishers 1991.

[30] Libronix Digital Library System; The Bible Knowledge Commentary. Logos Bible Software. The King James Version. Passage Guide: Genesis 15:17-18.

Additional Reference Materials

I Hate My Life: Winning the War Against Covetousness & *Discontent.* By Bishop Jacqueline E. McCullough. J.E. McCullough, LLC, Proclamation Publishing, 2019.

The Other Side of This. By Bishop Jacqueline E. McCullough. Bright Light Publishing Company, 2011.

Vanity: The Futility of a Self-Absorbed Life. Compiled Messages by Rev. Dr. Patricia McLeod. Bright Light Publishing Company, 2020.

Christian Discipleship 101: Don't Skip the Class! Compiled Messages by Rev. Dr. Patricia McLeod. Bright Light Publishing Company. Anticipated Release: June 2020.

Prophetic Crack: Pushers in the Pulpit / Addicts in the Pews. By Bishop Julia McMillan. Yorkshire Publishing Company, 2010.

Developing God's Leaders. By Rev. Dr. Robyn C. Edwards. Bright light Publishers, 2013.

Unthreatened – A Godly Man Under Female Leadership. By Pastor Terry Scott McMillan. Published by Terry Scott McMillan, 2019.

CPSIA information can be obtained
at www.ICGtesting.com
Printed in the USA
BVHW031914130920
588749BV00001B/39